The Complete Homework Planner

The Staff of the Princeton Review

PrincetonReview.com

Penguin
Random
House

The Princeton Review
110 East 42nd St, 7th Floor
New York, NY 10017

Published in the United States by Penguin Random
House, LLC, New York.

The Princeton Review is not affiliated with Princeton
University.

ISBN: 978-0-593-51652-2

Editors: Aaron Riccio and Laura Rose
Production Editors: Sarah Litt and Nina Mozes
Production Artist: Deborah Weber

Printed in China.

10 9 8 7 6 5 4 3 2 1

1st Edition

The Princeton Review Publishing Team
Rob Franek, Editor-in-Chief
David Soto, Senior Director, Data Operations
Stephen Koch, Senior Manager, Data Operations
Deborah Weber, Director of Production
Jason Ullmeyer, Production Design Manager
Jennifer Chapman, Senior Production Artist
Selena Coppock, Director of Editorial
Orion McBean, Senior Editor
Aaron Riccio, Senior Editor
Meave Shelton, Senior Editor
Chris Chimera, Editor
Patricia Murphy, Editor
Laura Rose, Editor

Penguin Random House Publishing Team
Tom Russell, VP, Publisher
Alison Stoltzfus, Senior Director, Publishing
Brett Wright, Senior Editor
Emily Hoffman, Assistant Managing Editor
Ellen Reed, Production Manager
Suzanne Lee, Designer
Eugenia Lo, Publishing Assistant

For customer service, please contact
editorialsupport@review.com, and be
sure to include:

· full title of the book

· ISBN

· page number

Acknowledgments

This unique book would not have been possible without the tips and suggestions and advice from the whole team at The Princeton Review. A debt of gratitude to our bold Director of Production, Deborah Weber, for helping to visually realize so many different elements, and to our production editors Sarah Litt and Nina Mozes for their invaluable questions and insights into how it was all fitting together. Thanks as well to our partners at Penguin Random House for working with us to address this homework-planning need. The editors of this book, who you can reach at editorialsupport@review.com, look forward hearing how you've refined your process.

Contents

Get More (**Free**) Content

at **PrincetonReview.com/prep**

As easy as **1·2·3**

1 Go to PrincetonReview.com/prep or scan the **QR code** and enter the following ISBN for your book: **9780593516522**

2 Answer a few simple questions to set up an exclusive Princeton Review account. *(If you already have one, you can just log in.)*

3 Enjoy access to your **FREE** content!

Once you've registered, you can...

- Access a free, full-length practice SAT and/or ACT

- Get valuable advice about the college application process, if needed, including tips for applying for financial aid

- Check to see if there have been any corrections or updates to this edition

- Print out additional copies of many of the worksheets and planner pages in this book for reuse

Need to report a potential **content** issue?

Contact **EditorialSupport@review.com** and include:

- full title of the book
- ISBN
- page number

Need to report a **technical** issue?

Contact **TPRStudentTech@review.com** and provide:

- your full name
- email address used to register the book
- full book title and ISBN
- Operating system (Mac/PC) and browser (Chrome, Firefox, Safari, etc.)

Introduction

You learn many things in school, but one thing that's never directly taught is how to approach your assignments and manage your workload. Students are just expected to get everything done, *or else*—and that's where *The Complete Homework Planner* comes in. The goal of this book is to help you create an organizational plan that's specific not only to your classes and schedule but customized to your needs as a learner. The activities, planners, and trackers in this book serve as templates to help you figure out how to complete your homework and studying without giving up either your sleep or social life. They are designed for you to personalize, expand upon, and apply at any grade level.

The majority of this book is broken up into two-page spreads. The left-hand pages consist of instructions, suggestions, and tips while the right-hand pages contain material for you to fill in. Additional copies of these planner pages can be printed from your free online student tools.

Here are how the various sections of this book function:

ACTIVITIES

Chapters 1, 2, and 3 will cultivate your ability to manage time, prioritize tasks, and study. We won't say that we've tried to put the "fun" in these fundamental skills—at the end of the day, it's work, and it should be treated as such—but we have done our best to come up with fresh ways to approach and visualize these concepts so that they might inspire you to look anew at your old habits. For your inspiration, we've filled out some samples of these pages that you can find at the back of the book and online in your free student tools.

These activities break up each task into three core strategies. You can easily identify them on the left-hand pages with the following icons:

 Free up more time in your life by completing this step.

 Be more efficient with your work by completing this step.

 Find ways to relax by completing this step.

PLANNERS

Chapters 4, 5, and 6 provide calendar planner pages for day-to-day activities, weekly schedules, and long-term monthly projects. The left-hand pages feature more granular breakdowns and specific tips to help you visualize your priorities and progress. The minutes you spend filling in these pages can save you hours of stress down the road, and as with any skill, the more you practice your planning, the more efficient you'll become. Use these pages to try a variety of methods for managing your time and review your notes to see which ones worked best.

SUBJECT PLANNERS

Chapter 7 focuses on the kinds of projects you'll receive, from science labs to research papers and group projects. These pages offer creative ways to help you improve how you study, approach tasks, and prioritize problems according to the subject matter. Simple images are included to help you build associations with these tools and concepts.

TRACKERS

If you've ever looked at the data behind a scientific trial, you know that hundreds of cases are studied over a period of time before any conclusions are drawn. Implementing a reliable homework system for yourself is *also* a science, and this section provides you with a means of collecting informative data about your habits (and those of your teachers) that you can use to improve not just your immediate workload, but also what you'll have on your plate in the semesters to come. Seeing is believing, as they say, so give yourself that visual edge.

HERE'S TO YOU

Unlike other planners, *The Complete Homework Planner* puts you actively in the driver's seat. You're not just filling in the same old dates over and over again, hoping for something to improve. Instead, you're taking each assignment to heart and learning from your biggest stressors and hardest projects so that each day, your workload becomes more manageable. So, here's to you, and the good habits and lifelong skills you'll build with this planner. We're here rooting for you every day, week, month, and year of your journey.

Chapter 1
Time Management

It can be hard to sit down and do homework, especially after a long day of school. Down time, a social life, or a part-time job seem more important. But homework serves the valuable purpose of reinforcing what you're learning in class, identifying where further practice may help, and yes, preparing you for those dreaded tests.

That's why it's important to manage your time, so you can get the work done *and* still sleep and have a social life. The activities in this section are designed to help you start identifying and reducing the points where you procrastinate and to establish routines that should give you more time for all your tasks. As you get better with planning, you might even be able to add a new extracurricular or pursue a hobby you're passionate about.

AVOIDING PROCRASTINATION

You can probably name a dozen things you'd rather be doing right this minute. (We appreciate you sticking with this book!) However, there's no way to get back the time you waste thinking about what you could be doing, and if you put off an assignment, it's only going to pile up for later. For an assignment of your choosing, fill out the card on the next page and write down how long it took you to do so. As you repeat this exercise and improve your habits, you should notice you're saving more time overall than you're spending up front. Over time, this should help you see the time you're saving by getting focused.

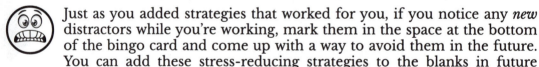

Use the Bingo card on the next page to help you identify things you can do to minimize distractions and focus on the work at hand. Some of the most tried-and-true suggestions are already filled in, and you can add your own tried-and-true tricks for concentrating in the blank spaces. Other squares on the Bingo card are common distractors: if they're *not* bothering you, write down why and check them off. If they *are*, write down how to avoid them, take your own advice, and then check them off.

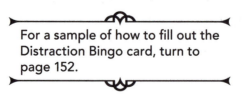

Just as you added strategies that worked for you, if you notice any *new* distractors while you're working, mark them in the space at the bottom of the bingo card and come up with a way to avoid them in the future. You can add these stress-reducing strategies to the blanks in future rounds of Distraction Bingo. Once you're set, check off as many items as you can, and when you've got at least five boxes marked in a row, start working. Remember, leaving yourself unfinished work or trying to rush through projects is only going to increase your stress, so do yourself—and your grades and overall comprehension of the subject—a favor and stay on task.

For a sample of how to fill out the Distraction Bingo card, turn to page 152.

✏ DISTRACTION BINGO

Time to Fill Out Card

Time to Complete Assignment

B	I	N	G	O
HUNGRY		Put away (or turned off) electronics	Limited outside noise in workspace	Tidied desk
Took a relaxing stretch	Turned off social media notifications	SITTING UNCOMFORTABLY		
Organized assignments by priority	CHECKING EMAIL	⭐ Focus		Finished chores
	Brightened the room		Gathered all materials needed for work	WATCHING TV
	Silenced phone		SLEEPY	

NEW DISTRACTORS	HOW TO AVOID THEM

WAYS TO READ

The amount of time you spend reading each night will depend on a variety of factors:

- difficulty (subject matter, word choice, density)
- genre (fiction, nonfiction, textbook)
- note-taking (light, heavy)

Over the next week, take some reading samples from various classes and use the calculators to the right to time yourself per page. This will give you an idea of how long, on average, you'll need to set aside for future assignments. This isn't about trying to speed read: it's about knowing how much time you need to absorb a text so that you can leave yourself enough time to read *without* rushing. Here are some approaches to be mindful of:

1. Skimming the Page

Skimming is the fastest way to read a page, but it can lead you to miss the finer points and details. If you're already comfortable with the material and only need a general overview of the subject, this technique can help. Time how long it takes you to skim a page and be honest: if you can't recall *any* of what you just read, then you didn't actually read it.

2. Reading the Full Page

Reading the full page is exactly what it sounds like. See how long it takes you to read everything on a page. You can then use this number to estimate how long it would take you to read x number of pages. Keep in mind, some material is denser than other material, which is why you should time yourself on several different subjects. You should also pay attention to things like font and page size, or the amount of non-text in a book, so that you don't underestimate future assignments.

3. Active Reading

Actively reading is the most comprehensive way to digest material. You're not only reading, but also highlighting and taking notes. This will help you when it comes time to answer questions or write an essay about what you've read. Make sure you're only focusing on the important parts of the text, like keywords (which you can later make into flashcards) or content you think will come up on an exam or in class. If you're not pressed for time now, or know that you'll need to save time later, this is a great approach.

✎ READING CALCULATOR

	FICTION	TEXTBOOK	NONFICTION
	_____ (title)	_____ (title)	_____ (title)
	_____ (subject)	_____ (subject)	_____ (subject)
1. SKIMMING THE PAGE	☐ pages ☐ minutes _____ page(s)/minute	☐ pages ☐ minutes _____ page(s)/minute	☐ pages ☐ minutes _____ page(s)/minute
2. READING THE FULL PAGE	☐ pages ☐ minutes _____ page(s)/minute	☐ pages ☐ minutes _____ page(s)/minute	☐ pages ☐ minutes _____ page(s)/minute
3. ACTIVE READING	☐ pages ☐ minutes _____ page(s)/minute	☐ pages ☐ minutes _____ page(s)/minute	☐ pages ☐ minutes _____ page(s)/minute

Remember, to find these rates, divide the number of pages you read by the number of minutes it took.

$$\frac{\boxed{}\ \text{pages}}{\boxed{}\ \text{minutes}} = \underline{\quad} \text{ page(s)/minute}$$

If you've repeated this across multiple days, take the *average* of those rates by adding them together and dividing by the number of days. This will give you an increasingly accurate prediction.

Turn to page 153 to see a sample of a filled out Reading Calculator.

TYPES OF WRITING

Because open-ended responses are unique, begin each writing assignment by setting a baseline for what obstacles you expect to face.

- creative writing (generating ideas)
- argumentative writing (backing up your perspective)
- research-based writing (finding sources)

Find a variety of writing projects from different classes, because depending on your interests, you might find it easier to write about history than science. Record how much time you spend on each of the following tasks, and adjust future projects based on what's most efficient for you.

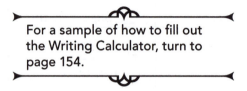

For a sample of how to fill out the Writing Calculator, turn to page 154.

Research

If you've made use of the Reading Calculator, you may already have an idea of how long this will take. It may seem as if you're spending extra time on preliminary work, but it should save you time in the long run.

Pre-writing

Perhaps a short stream-of-consciousness free-write (or a dictation into an app) will help loosen up your thoughts; maybe you prefer to generate an outline so that you can be sure that you connect all your ideas and answer the question in full.

Writing

Depending on the project and your writing style, you may not need to spend much time researching or pre-writing. But if you find yourself frequently getting writer's block or taking a long time here, try taking notes and generating rough content to see if helps.

Editing

Depending on how much time you have, set your work aside for an hour (or a day) and then review it. This is your last chance to improve your grade by making sure that you've included all the points you wanted to make and that they make sense. Even if you won't be penalized for it, make sure everything is spelled correctly; bad habits (and an over-reliance on spell-check) can be hard to break.

✎ WRITING CALCULATOR

Research ▤	Pre-Writing ▥	Writing ◩	Editing 〰

Once you know how long the entire project took, shade in the percent of the whole spent on each portion; e.g., 30% + 20% + 25% + 25%.

CREATIVE WRITING   Time Spent:

Researching: _____ minutes   Writing: _____ minutes

Pre-Writing: _____ minutes   Editing: _____ minutes

Total: _____ words and _____ pages in _____ minutes

0%   10%   20%   30%   40%   50%   60%   70%   80%   90%   100%

ARGUMENTATIVE WRITING   Time Spent:

Researching: _____ minutes   Writing: _____ minutes

Pre-Writing: _____ minutes   Editing: _____ minutes

Total: _____ words and _____ pages in _____ minutes

0%   10%   20%   30%   40%   50%   60%   70%   80%   90%   100%

RESEARCH-BASED WRITING   Time Spent:

Researching: _____ minutes   Writing: _____ minutes

Pre-Writing: _____ minutes   Editing: _____ minutes

Total: _____ words and _____ pages in _____ minutes

0%   10%   20%   30%   40%   50%   60%   70%   80%   90%   100%

MATH PROBLEMS

Though the calculator to the right uses the terms "easy" and "hard," know that no two students find the *same* math problems to be equally difficult. Additionally, even an easy question can be time-consuming if there are a lot of steps and opportunities to make errors. Your first task, therefore, is to define which subjects or types of problems you find difficult. Then, as you work through a homework assignment, note how long a question you thought would be simple (or challenging) takes.

Adjust your categorizations as needed: if a multiple-step long-division problem consistently takes longer than a quadratic equation but you've sorted them as easy and hard, change your groupings around. Revisit your rankings as you continue to hone your math skills, work with tutors, and learn new techniques. Try to reduce the amount of time the questions take across the board.

As you improve your homework-solving speed, you'll also be doing better on your tests—especially timed ones. Do be aware, however, that you might not be allowed to use a calculator or equation sheet on every assignment or exam, and that could result in slower solving times. Circle the indicated icons for questions potentially involving a calculator or equation sheet and consider if that may have helped you.

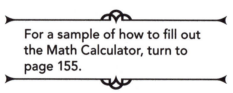

For a sample of how to fill out the Math Calculator, turn to page 155.

✎ MATH CALCULATOR

TYPES OF PROBLEMS		
EASY	**MEDIUM**	**HARD**

Calculator

			Equation Sheet	
✗ ✔	1. ____ Minutes Taken		✗ ✔
✗ ✔	2. ____ Minutes Taken		✗ ✔
✗ ✔	3. ____ Minutes Taken		✗ ✔
✗ ✔	4. ____ Minutes Taken		✗ ✔
✗ ✔	5. ____ Minutes Taken		✗ ✔
✗ ✔	6. ____ Minutes Taken		✗ ✔
✗ ✔	7. ____ Minutes Taken		✗ ✔
✗ ✔	8. ____ Minutes Taken		✗ ✔
✗ ✔	9. ____ Minutes Taken		✗ ✔
✗ ✔	10. ____ Minutes Taken		✗ ✔

Chapter 2

Prioritizing Tasks

Where you do your work, and when, matters. Over the course of this chapter, experiment with doing your work in a variety of places and at different times and see what's most efficient for you. Then, based on your goals, try to turn your best practices into a routine.

NECESSARY TOOLS

 There's an old joke about a diner who calls the waiter over to complain about the soup. The waiter asks if it is too hot. The customer tells him to taste it. The waiter questions whether it's seasoned improperly. The patron pauses and repeats: "Taste it." The waiter, frustrated, asks if it's the wrong order. Again, the diner requests that the waiter just taste it. Finally, the waiter agrees... and then pauses: "Where's the spoon?" he asks. "Aha!" replies the customer. It's hard to eat soup without a spoon, and it's hard to do your homework without a pencil, so don't waste time—know what you need, however simple, and make sure you have it.

 Now you are ready to break down your assignment into manageable tasks. You can do this by creating an overall checklist for each subject, but don't forget to review your checklist to make sure you didn't leave out any special requirements.

 To know what you need, you need to know what the assignment is asking. Begin by scanning your assignment and seeing the format and what the questions call for. If it's a series of math problems, find out if you'll need a calculator, a compass, or any other formula. If it's chemistry, make sure you have the periodic table at the ready. You can save a lot of time by having all of the physical tools that you will need accessible and ready to use. Fill in the tools that you'll need for this project in the boxes in the backpack.

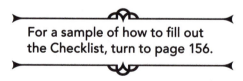
For a sample of how to fill out the Checklist, turn to page 156.

✎ CHECKLIST

Name of Class: _____

Type of Assignment: _____

TASK	REQUIREMENTS	DONE

PHYSICAL TOOLS NEEDED

DISCOVER YOUR TASKS

It's important to be able to sift through extraneous material to make sure you find exactly what your instructor is asking for. The workspace word search puzzle on the next page is good practice. In this type of puzzle, words read either across, down, or diagonally, and may be reversed. See how quickly you can find the words indicated in each of the following three steps.

 There are five words provided below the grid on the next page. Write down how long it took to find them. Consider whether it was easier to find long words or short words—make sure you're not tripped up by small details, or by objects that look *close* to being right.

 There are yet another five common homework-related objects which have *not* been given. Write down what each of them are and how long it took to find them and consider whether it's more difficult to find something when you *don't* know what you're looking for.

 There are another five images provided, each of which corresponds to the name of an object that is also hidden in the grid. Note that to find the object, you have to first organize it by spelling out what that word was—and you have to correctly identify it: if LAMP isn't there, is there maybe another word that would work? Write down how long these items took as well.

This word search wasn't included just to provide a fun break from the worksheets. If you look at how long each set took to find, you'll probably agree that when you have a clear list of tasks to find (or do), it's much easier to sort through the distractions and disorganization to complete it.

The answers to this word search can be found on page 157.

✎ WORKSPACE WORD SEARCH

R	C	C	D	I	C	T	I	O	N	A	R	Y	P
Y	E	K	T	F	A	N	R	S	N	U	D	O	M
L	T	S	K	O	O	L	A	N	N	E	T	N	R
C	E	U	E	N	K	L	E	E	S	K	P	R	C
K	T	D	R	A	H	P	D	P	S	T	O	A	R
I	A	C	C	L	R	P	N	E	U	R	L	A	E
N	C	B	O	A	P	C	D	N	R	C	S	T	N
O	C	E	O	M	C	C	H	R	U	L	T	T	E
T	M	N	E	P	O	T	E	L	I	A	P	T	P
E	R	A	S	E	R	T	A	C	L	D	O	L	R
S	K	O	O	B	N	T	N	S	N	A	T	P	A
L	E	S	O	I	O	E	E	L	R	U	P	I	H
P	N	D	R	R	P	K	K	T	O	Y	A	R	S
H	K	P	O	R	E	L	P	A	T	S	L	O	I

Provided Words	Missing Words	Images
DICTIONARY		
DESKTOP		
NOTES		
PENS		
RESEARCH		

BALANCE YOUR WORKLOAD

There are variable exercises in this planner because every student has their own strengths (and weaknesses). Begin by pinpointing what you feel are your particular skills (time-management, focus, etc.) and subject-area interests.

 Write each of your assignments for the given day in the middle column. Use the calculators from Chapter 1 to estimate how long they'll take. Once you know how much work you've got overall, you can take a deep breath and start taking it piece by piece.

 For each assignment, choose the ranking of each category (time, stress, and organization) that sums it up. Enter the total (a number between 3 and 12) in the "points" box.

 Keeping in mind your strengths and estimates, assign each project a priority—you'll do 1 first, then 2, then 3, and so on. This is a bit like making a balanced meal so that you don't upset your homework "stomach": are you likelier to succeed by starting with a light and easy "dessert" of a task or should you dig into the meatiest project first, while you're at your hungriest? As you work later into the evening, ask yourself whether there's work that you feel so comfortable with that you can practically do it in your sleep.

The way in which doctors prioritize patients is known as triage. In short: they do the most critical, necessary tasks first. This doesn't mean that the other work isn't important, only that it can sit a little bit longer before failing. If you don't have time to do everything on your list, make sure you're at least completing the ones that will have the greatest impact on your grade.

✎ KNOW YOUR STRENGTHS

Strengths	Interests

PRIORITY	POINTS	ASSIGNMENTS	TIME
☐	☐		
☐	☐		
☐	☐		

Time	Stress	Organization
1. Due soon, low impact	**1.** Do it in my sleep	**1.** Can do at school
2. Due soon, high impact	**2.** Need a little focus	**2.** Can do on commute
3. Due now, low impact	**3.** Need a lot of focus	**3.** Can do at home
4. Due now, high impact	**4.** Struggling with subject	**4.** Must do at library/ other

For a sample of how to fill out this worksheet, turn to page 158.

REVIEW YOUR MISTAKES

You're technically done with homework when you hand it in, but if you stop there, you're only making future projects for that teacher harder on yourself. Instead, use this activity to review the notes you get back so that you can improve.

 Begin by transferring your errors to the worksheet on the right. This doesn't mean copying down what the teacher wrote word for word. Instead, get to the heart of the error and state as clearly as possible what you did wrong. Evaluate the type of mistake:

  1 = A simple mistake, like a calculation error or typo.
  2 = A comprehension error, like misreading and giving the wrong answer.
  3 = A technique issue, like not showing your work or fully explaining yourself.
  4 = A content issue, like not understanding the material.

If you keep making the *same* mistake, increase the value of that error by +1, as those represent more severe bad habits that should be addressed.

 Once you've tallied up the various errors, use the "Ways to Improve" column to plan out what you can do to better prepare in the future. If that means you must reread a section of text or review and solve more problems, find time for doing so. Your goal is to adjust or develop your homework-solving strategies, not to just keep trying the same thing over and over (unless it's working for you). Look at some of the tips throughout this book, and consider speaking to classmates, your teacher, or a tutor if you're stuck. Once you feel that you know how to resolve a given error, cross out its number.

 On the scale at the bottom of the page, you're going to put two numbers. On the left, put the total of the errors you evaluated, divided by a class score of 3 (if you're doing well), 2 (if you're struggling), or 1 (if you're failing). On the right, add up all the numbers not crossed out. The left score represents how much of an impact the errors you're making may have on your overall grade. If the right score is greater in value, consider trying to resolve more errors first so that you can safely move on.

✎ BALANCE YOUR WEAKNESSES

Teacher: _____ Subject: _____

Assignment Date: _____ Score: _____

TYPE	ERRORS	WAYS TO IMPROVE
☐		
☐		
☐		
☐		
☐		
☐		
☐		
☐		

☐ *Total*

☐ *Class Score*

For a sample of how to fill out this worksheet, turn to page 159.

MAKE PROJECTS MANAGEABLE

 Big projects can seem intimidating at first glance. Begin by making sure you understand the project assignment and its timeline. Then define the scope so you stay within its bounds. So-called "scope creep" (or, more amusingly, "kitchen-sink syndrome") sets in when you keep adding to your initial plan, and can lower the quality of your finished product—or, worse, keep you from finishing it on schedule.

To avoid this, stick to the parameters of what you need. Identify and collect your supplies and make any reservations you may need, such as time in a computer lab or library, or space in a classroom. If you are working with others, schedule meeting times, and if you are relying on outside contributors, whether that's for an interview or a component, set up appointments well in advance, with enough time to reschedule if needed.

 Look at the big picture and identify parts of the task. Now think about a logical order of completing each of these chunks and create a realistic timeline. "Realistic" in this case means that it's accounting for real-world interruptions, like illness, bad weather, or unexpected conflicts.

If you're working with a team, know each member's strengths and weaknesses. It's important that you communicate with each other and make decisions together to build trust. After all, this is a group effort, and everyone should play an equal part in its success. That may mean compromising on certain aspects: something that takes you an extra hour but saves everybody else multiple hours is probably worth it, and you'll be glad when you're on the receiving end of that help.

 Before you can transfer information over to the appropriate planner pages, you'll want to build out a mini-calendar here of meetings associated with this project. This will help you confirm that things are spaced out throughout the project—having all your meetings the first week might not be the best idea. Instead, build them around your deadlines, so you (or your team) can follow up.

✏️ BUILD A PROJECT WORKSHEET

Project: _____

Due Date: _____

Team Members: _____

_____

Outside Contributors: _____

_____

Reservations Needed: _____

Materials Needed: _____

_____

_____

Chunk	Order	Assigned Team Member	Deadline

Meeting Dates	Reservation Dates	Appointments	
		Contact	Time

For a sample of how to fill out the Build a Project Worksheet, turn to page 160.

Chapter 3
Study Aids

Not all homework assignments are meant to be finished in a single night. As you organize your workload, look for ways to spread that work across multiple days, and look for opportunities to check in on and refresh your knowledge throughout the week as opposed to waiting for the last minute to start thinking about how to approach a project.

NEED TO KNOW SHEET

It's a good idea to keep some sort of sheet on hand of commonly used content for a class, especially if you keep forgetting it. Think of these terms as items in a toolbox or a first aid kit: you don't always need them, but you don't want to waste time searching for them when you do.

Create a tracker for each subject (or topic, if you want to get that granular); you can print additional copies of this sheet from your free online Student Tools or write out your own. This can be a list of keywords, critical dates, or equations. In short, whenever you learn a new concept you'll frequently refer back to, add it.

Get in the habit of transferring the most important notes either before or after you do your homework. If you feel confident that you've memorized something on your list, or you know that the class has moved on to an entirely different field and that material won't be tested again, put a checkmark next to that item so that you don't waste time looking at those entries when you're doing future assignments.

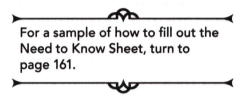

For a sample of how to fill out the Need to Know Sheet, turn to page 161.

✏ NEED TO KNOW SHEET

Name of Class _____

SUBJECT OR TOPIC	NEED TO KNOW

CREATING FLASHCARDS

Flashcards are great study aids because they help you test your knowledge and reinforce ideas. They are a highly effective means of transferring information from short-term to long-term memory through repetition, which means you'll want to use these cards frequently. Take inspiration from the sample template on the next page to design your own deck of flashcards and use them to think not only about how to memorize material for a test but how to complete upcoming projects.

Begin by marking the right-hand box of each card with the subject (you can abbreviate). At first, try working through only those flashcards associated with a single class. Later, try mixing in those from other subjects as well.

Keep the "flash" part of flashcards in mind as you work; choose short, direct prompts. Don't dwell on these flashcards as you fill them out; the idea is that you'll keep returning to the prompt with fresh eyes and new ways to answer it. You'll save time by prompting your unconscious mind to keep thinking about these flashcards between sessions. Once you're confident that you've mastered a card, put a checkmark on the front and remove it from your deck. Hold on to these completed cards and cycle them back in periodically, just to be sure.

Flashcards help minimize stress because they're bite-sized tasks. They also allow you to retrieve information over the course of multiple waves. The sample flashcard on the next page was designed to leave you with space to fill in a card over time, putting concepts into your own words (or pictures) and sparking and fleshing out ideas to make sure you're fully prepared when you sit down for a test or your homework. See how your answer to the prompt on the front of the card may have changed from what you originally had on the top, or in any of the other filled in boxes. Add any new ideas, or if you're stuck, try putting your answer in new words or as pictures. Remember, these cards are just a suggestion—design your deck in the way that's most helpful for you.

To view a sample flashcard, turn to page 162.

✎ SAMPLE FLASHCARDS

FRONT

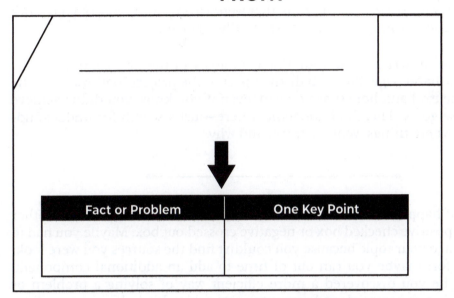

BACK

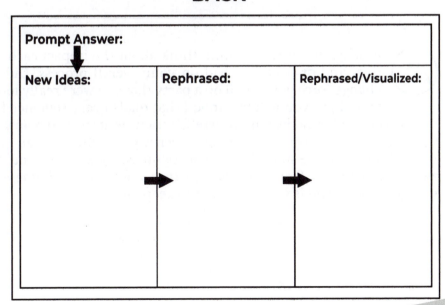

BEST-LAID PLANS

Just as it is good practice to compare your planned goals against your overall schedule while you're working on a project so that you can stay on task, so too is it useful to do the same once the project is complete. In a post-mortem, you compare what you *intended* to do against what you *actually* did and draw conclusions about how to either fix something that went wrong or to modify your work to incorporate something that was unexpectedly efficient.

 Begin by writing out your intended goals in the first column on the right-hand page. Put each distinct part of the project in its own box. Be as neutral and honest as you can, even if you know you didn't achieve these goals. There's no judgement here—just a search for understanding where things went off-track, and why.

 Stuff happens! In the middle column, fill out what happened in either the positive checked box or negative crossed out box. Maybe you had to change your topic because you couldn't find the sources you were looking for; maybe you ran out of time to add an additional component. Maybe you discovered a more efficient way of solving a problem or looking up material, and you cut your workload in half.

Finally, in the last column, think about the impact each of these positives and/or negatives had on your overall process. Did a last-minute change force you to bail on a party that you were really looking forward to and put you in a bad mood that made every sentence feel like it was taking forever? Or did leaving yourself extra time at the end help you reorganize things in a timely fashion? Write down what you would change in the future to make things go more smoothly—what goes in the box is what you'd literally take away (like leftovers from a restaurant that you're taking home with you), and what goes on the lid is what you want to keep out.

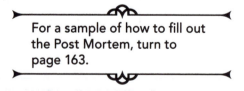

For a sample of how to fill out the Post Mortem, turn to page 163.

✎ POST MORTEM

INTENT	RESULT	TAKEAWAY

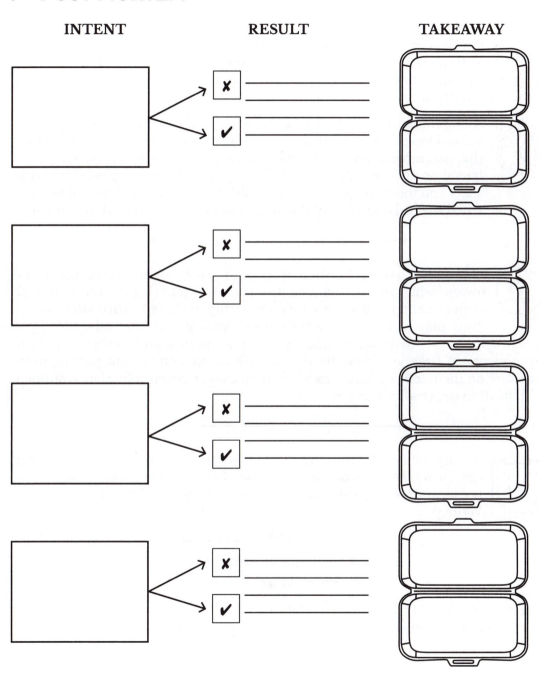

LOOK AT YOUR WORK WITH FRESH EYES

You know who is really good at organizing things for each of your classes? Your teachers. (That's not to say they can't make mistakes—if you have questions at the end of a class or with the homework, jot it down and try to get it answered while it's still fresh in your mind or while there's still time for you to finish the project correctly.) For the most part, however, the assignments you get are going to be time-tested and aligned with the needs of the class.

 Along those lines, then, it can sometimes help to do a bit of role-reversal and look at your work as if *you* were the teacher. When you first get the assignment, try explaining each part of it to someone else like a friend or a parent. Ideally, do this without looking at the original worksheet and then compare what you said to what's on the sheet. Make sure you didn't miss anything! Put your notes into the Prework rectangle.

 Then, once you're finished with your work, switch roles again and review what you've "handed in" with a teacher's eye. Look at each response and jot down what it's answering. If there's a mismatch, something may be off. Be honest here—it's your grade, after all—and if you see an opportunity to fix something and get more points, do so, especially if you have plenty of time left. Your future self will thank you for not putting more pressure on them to keep their grade up when they're potentially *more* swamped. Fill this into the Draft rectangle.

 Finally, when you've gotten your assignment *back* from the teacher, don't just take the grade at face value. "Become" your teacher again and try to understand why questions were wrong or where they fell short. Write your notes down in the Grading rectangle.

See the sample on page 164.

Use the Teacher Tracker (on page 149) to write down any specific habits you notice about an individual teacher, particularly with regard to how harshly they grade your work or what they *don't* take off credit for. This will help you better make judgement calls about how to get a better grade in this and any future classes with that teacher.

✎ BE THE TEACHER

Prework	Draft	Grading

Chapter 4

Daily Planner

Think of your daily planner a bit like a to-do list. In most cases, this means prioritizing the work that you're going to have to hand in tomorrow. If you're finding yourself overwhelmed with work, look further ahead to the future in your weekly and monthly planners to better distribute your assignments. If you can't, be certain that all of the classes you're taking are necessary.

DAILY TASK BREAKDOWN

Begin by filling in the "Classes" column on your day planner to the right with your class schedule for that day. Draw a box around any class that extends from one hourly block to the next. Just make sure to leave space between classes, because those gaps are where you might be able to get some work done. In the "Homework" column, then fill in which assignments you're going to do. Bear in mind where you'll physically be—on a commute, by the library—so that you can slot in the appropriate assignments for the places you'll be. You can slot homework for yourself in the shaded boxes—or for hours outside this range—but be mindful of how this will impact your sleep schedule.

Student Example: Alan loves to draw. When he asked his friends what they believed to be his strengths, they all said he was creative, easy-going, and the person they go to for design advice. He is a somewhat slow reader and really struggles with writing paragraphs. Math and science are okay, but he dislikes rote memorization. He received an award at a student art show recently and is creating backdrops for an upcoming student stage production.

Alan prefers to do more difficult tasks first. He also wants to organize the tasks by priority, with the highest priority first. He used the calculators from Chapter 1 to determine the approximate amount of time he needed for each task. Here is Alan's planner page:

TASK	PRIORITY (1–4)	TIME NEEDED
History—read pages 98–132	1	0:50
English—read pages 45–68 of Macbeth	1	1:00
Algebra II Trig, Chapter 3, problems 1–18	1	0:50
Chemistry—complete Lab 4	2	1:30
Art and Design—draw a face that is happy	3	0:45
Study for a test on soccer rules	4	0:30

Alan likes to work at home. For his reading assignments he prefers to have access to a computer in case he needs to look something up. For math, science, and art he likes to sit at a desk, and while studying he prefers to sit in a comfortable chair. He's managed his time, organized his tasks by interest and priority, and identified his workspace. By having a plan that works for him Alan is confident that he can stay on track to get the tasks done.

✏ DAILY PLANNER

Day _____		
	Classes	**Homework**
7:00 A.M.–8:00 A.M.		
8:00 A.M.–9:00 A.M.		
9:00 A.M.–10:00 A.M.		
10:00 A.M.–11:00 A.M.		
11:00 A.M.–12:00 P.M.		
12:00 P.M.–1:00 P.M.		
1:00 P.M.–2:00 P.M.		
2:00 P.M.–3:00 P.M.		
3:00 P.M.–4:00 P.M.		
4:00 P.M.–5:00 P.M.		
5:00 P.M.–6:00 P.M.		
6:00 P.M.–7:00 P.M.		
7:00 P.M.–8:00 P.M.		
8:00 P.M.–9:00 P.M.		
9:00 P.M.–10:00 P.M.		
10:00 P.M.–11:00 P.M.		
11:00 P.M.–12:00 A.M.		
12:00 A.M.–1:00 A.M.		
1:00 A.M.–2:00 A.M.		

Total Time Spent on Homework

DAILY TASK BREAKDOWN

It is worth re-emphasizing why the hours of 9:00 P.M. to 2:00 A.M. are shaded, and why the hours of 2:00 A.M. to 7:00 A.M. do not appear. This doesn't mean that you can't use that time if needed, but we don't recommend it. Sleep is important, and consistently working past 9:00 P.M. can burn you out. Make a record of how much sleep you got and tally those up on another sheet (see the Sleep Tracker on page 141). If your assignments are taking you longer than usual and your sleep numbers are low, there's likely a connection there that you should address as soon as possible.

TASK	PRIORITY (1–4)	TIME NEEDED

Make sure you fully understand the assignment when you get it. To be sure, look at the questions and try paraphrasing them, or identifying the formulas you might need. If you're stuck, try to ask the teacher for clarification as soon as possible.

✏ DAILY PLANNER

Day _____		
	Classes	**Homework**
7:00 A.M.–8:00 A.M.		
8:00 A.M.–9:00 A.M.		
9:00 A.M.–10:00 A.M.		
10:00 A.M.–11:00 A.M.		
11:00 A.M.–12:00 P.M.		
12:00 P.M.–1:00 P.M.		
1:00 P.M.–2:00 P.M.		
2:00 P.M.–3:00 P.M.		
3:00 P.M.–4:00 P.M.		
4:00 P.M.–5:00 P.M.		
5:00 P.M.–6:00 P.M.		
6:00 P.M.–7:00 P.M.		
7:00 P.M.–8:00 P.M.		
8:00 P.M.–9:00 P.M.		
9:00 P.M.–10:00 P.M.		
10:00 P.M.–11:00 P.M.		
11:00 P.M.–12:00 A.M.		
12:00 A.M.–1:00 A.M.		
1:00 A.M.–2:00 A.M.		

Total Time Spent on Homework

DAILY TASK BREAKDOWN

There's space on each daily planner for you to look at the total amount of work you've done on a given day, and you shouldn't just forget about those numbers. Try transferring those numbers to another sheet (see the Work Tracker on page 143) and keep an eye out for unusually high results. If your workload is consistently overwhelming and you've already tried the strategies in this book, you might want to speak to your teachers to find out how much time they expect a particular assignment to take. You could also adjust your next semester's classes or speak to an academic advisor about your options.

TASK	PRIORITY (1–4)	TIME NEEDED

There's nothing wrong with asking for an extension— but don't assume that you'll get one. And try not to wait until the last minute to ask! More importantly, remember that you'll still have to do that work, so if you expect to be even busier in the future, try to avoid letting assignments accumulate.

✏ DAILY PLANNER

Day _____	Classes	Homework
7:00 A.M.–8:00 A.M.		
8:00 A.M.–9:00 A.M.		
9:00 A.M.–10:00 A.M.		
10:00 A.M.–11:00 A.M.		
11:00 A.M.–12:00 P.M.		
12:00 P.M.–1:00 P.M.		
1:00 P.M.–2:00 P.M.		
2:00 P.M.–3:00 P.M.		
3:00 P.M.–4:00 P.M.		
4:00 P.M.–5:00 P.M.		
5:00 P.M.–6:00 P.M.		
6:00 P.M.–7:00 P.M.		
7:00 P.M.–8:00 P.M.		
8:00 P.M.–9:00 P.M.		
9:00 P.M.–10:00 P.M.		
10:00 P.M.–11:00 P.M.		
11:00 P.M.–12:00 A.M.		
12:00 A.M.–1:00 A.M.		
1:00 A.M.–2:00 A.M.		

Total Time Spent on Homework

DAILY TASK BREAKDOWN

Slot any assignments you have for tonight into this planner. Then use the appropriate Chapter 1 calculators to estimate the time you'll need and do the "Know Your Strengths" activity from Chapter 2 to determine the order in which to tackle the assignments. If some of tonight's work is a chunk of a larger project, add *only* the portion that you plan on doing (or the amount of time you want to spend getting through as much as you can) and refer to the week and month planners in the next chapters to be sure that you're staying on track.

TASK	PRIORITY (1–4)	TIME NEEDED

Create a checklist for anything the assignment requires, like sources or shown work, and mark off each item as you tackle it. Pay close attention to any material you may need to collect <u>before</u> you get home, whether from another person or a physical location like a library.

✎ DAILY PLANNER

Day _____	Classes	Homework
7:00 A.M.–8:00 A.M.		
8:00 A.M.–9:00 A.M.		
9:00 A.M.–10:00 A.M.		
10:00 A.M.–11:00 A.M.		
11:00 A.M.–12:00 P.M.		
12:00 P.M.–1:00 P.M.		
1:00 P.M.–2:00 P.M.		
2:00 P.M.–3:00 P.M.		
3:00 P.M.–4:00 P.M.		
4:00 P.M.–5:00 P.M.		
5:00 P.M.–6:00 P.M.		
6:00 P.M.–7:00 P.M.		
7:00 P.M.–8:00 P.M.		
8:00 P.M.–9:00 P.M.		
9:00 P.M.–10:00 P.M.		
10:00 P.M.–11:00 P.M.		
11:00 P.M.–12:00 A.M.		
12:00 A.M.–1:00 A.M.		
1:00 A.M.–2:00 A.M.		

Total Time Spent on Homework [ ]

DAILY TASK BREAKDOWN

Despite the name of this book, don't feel as if you must limit yourself only to homework in this planner. You should make a list of *all* the commitments you have and add them accordingly to your daily, weekly, and monthly planners as needed. To make sure you don't forget any, use the Commitment Tracker on page 145.

TASK	PRIORITY (1–4)	TIME NEEDED

If your assignment involves memorization, try the chunking method. Take individual pieces of information and group them into larger, connected units.

✐ DAILY PLANNER

Day _____		
	Classes	**Homework**
7:00 A.M.–8:00 A.M.		
8:00 A.M.–9:00 A.M.		
9:00 A.M.–10:00 A.M.		
10:00 A.M.–11:00 A.M.		
11:00 A.M.–12:00 P.M.		
12:00 P.M.–1:00 P.M.		
1:00 P.M.–2:00 P.M.		
2:00 P.M.–3:00 P.M.		
3:00 P.M.–4:00 P.M.		
4:00 P.M.–5:00 P.M.		
5:00 P.M.–6:00 P.M.		
6:00 P.M.–7:00 P.M.		
7:00 P.M.–8:00 P.M.		
8:00 P.M.–9:00 P.M.		
9:00 P.M.–10:00 P.M.		
10:00 P.M.–11:00 P.M.		
11:00 P.M.–12:00 A.M.		
12:00 A.M.–1:00 A.M.		
1:00 A.M.–2:00 A.M.		

**Total Time Spent
on Homework**

DAILY TASK BREAKDOWN

TASK	PRIORITY (1–4)	TIME NEEDED

When learning new words (or symbols), divide the total number that you want to memorize by the number of days you've been given to do so. (If you need to pick up 20 words in 5 days, focus on a manageable 4 each day.)

✎ DAILY PLANNER

Day _____	Classes	Homework
7:00 A.M.–8:00 A.M.		
8:00 A.M.–9:00 A.M.		
9:00 A.M.–10:00 A.M.		
10:00 A.M.–11:00 A.M.		
11:00 A.M.–12:00 P.M.		
12:00 P.M.–1:00 P.M.		
1:00 P.M.–2:00 P.M.		
2:00 P.M.–3:00 P.M.		
3:00 P.M.–4:00 P.M.		
4:00 P.M.–5:00 P.M.		
5:00 P.M.–6:00 P.M.		
6:00 P.M.–7:00 P.M.		
7:00 P.M.–8:00 P.M.		
8:00 P.M.–9:00 P.M.		
9:00 P.M.–10:00 P.M.		
10:00 P.M.–11:00 P.M.		
11:00 P.M.–12:00 A.M.		
12:00 A.M.–1:00 A.M.		
1:00 A.M.–2:00 A.M.		

Total Time Spent on Homework

DAILY TASK BREAKDOWN

TASK	PRIORITY (1–4)	TIME NEEDED

Sherlock Holmes used a "memory palace" to recall and connect a great many facts. If that works for you, great, but you can also create a physical version for yourself. A "mind map" is a diagram that focuses on a central topic and connects it to various sub-topics.

✏ DAILY PLANNER

Day _____		
	Classes	**Homework**
7:00 A.M.–8:00 A.M.		
8:00 A.M.–9:00 A.M.		
9:00 A.M.–10:00 A.M.		
10:00 A.M.–11:00 A.M.		
11:00 A.M.–12:00 P.M.		
12:00 P.M.–1:00 P.M.		
1:00 P.M.–2:00 P.M.		
2:00 P.M.–3:00 P.M.		
3:00 P.M.–4:00 P.M.		
4:00 P.M.–5:00 P.M.		
5:00 P.M.–6:00 P.M.		
6:00 P.M.–7:00 P.M.		
7:00 P.M.–8:00 P.M.		
8:00 P.M.–9:00 P.M.		
9:00 P.M.–10:00 P.M.		
10:00 P.M.–11:00 P.M.		
11:00 P.M.–12:00 A.M.		
12:00 A.M.–1:00 A.M.		
1:00 A.M.–2:00 A.M.		

Total Time Spent on Homework

DAILY TASK BREAKDOWN

TASK	PRIORITY (1–4)	TIME NEEDED

Your notes are <u>your</u> notes—nobody else needs to be able to read them. Use whatever abbreviations, symbols, and shorthand phrases work for you. That said, <u>you</u> still need to be able to read them, so don't be too brief.

✎ DAILY PLANNER

Day _____	Classes	Homework
7:00 A.M.–8:00 A.M.		
8:00 A.M.–9:00 A.M.		
9:00 A.M.–10:00 A.M.		
10:00 A.M.–11:00 A.M.		
11:00 A.M.–12:00 P.M.		
12:00 P.M.–1:00 P.M.		
1:00 P.M.–2:00 P.M.		
2:00 P.M.–3:00 P.M.		
3:00 P.M.–4:00 P.M.		
4:00 P.M.–5:00 P.M.		
5:00 P.M.–6:00 P.M.		
6:00 P.M.–7:00 P.M.		
7:00 P.M.–8:00 P.M.		
8:00 P.M.–9:00 P.M.		
9:00 P.M.–10:00 P.M.		
10:00 P.M.–11:00 P.M.		
11:00 P.M.–12:00 A.M.		
12:00 A.M.–1:00 A.M.		
1:00 A.M.–2:00 A.M.		

Total Time Spent on Homework

DAILY TASK BREAKDOWN

TASK	PRIORITY (1-4)	TIME NEEDED

You don't have to tackle an assignment all at once. This is especially useful if you're having trouble immediately coming up with a position or response. In those cases, let the material sit with you as you work on something else, and then come back to it.

✎ DAILY PLANNER

Day _____	Classes	Homework
7:00 A.M.–8:00 A.M.		
8:00 A.M.–9:00 A.M.		
9:00 A.M.–10:00 A.M.		
10:00 A.M.–11:00 A.M.		
11:00 A.M.–12:00 P.M.		
12:00 P.M.–1:00 P.M.		
1:00 P.M.–2:00 P.M.		
2:00 P.M.–3:00 P.M.		
3:00 P.M.–4:00 P.M.		
4:00 P.M.–5:00 P.M.		
5:00 P.M.–6:00 P.M.		
6:00 P.M.–7:00 P.M.		
7:00 P.M.–8:00 P.M.		
8:00 P.M.–9:00 P.M.		
9:00 P.M.–10:00 P.M.		
10:00 P.M.–11:00 P.M.		
11:00 P.M.–12:00 A.M.		
12:00 A.M.–1:00 A.M.		
1:00 A.M.–2:00 A.M.		

Total Time Spent on Homework

DAILY TASK BREAKDOWN

TASK	PRIORITY (1–4)	TIME NEEDED

Adjust, adjust, adjust. If an approach isn't working, try a new one. If a question has you stumped, move on and remember to come back to it.

✏️ DAILY PLANNER

Day _____		
	Classes	**Homework**
7:00 A.M.–8:00 A.M.		
8:00 A.M.–9:00 A.M.		
9:00 A.M.–10:00 A.M.		
10:00 A.M.–11:00 A.M.		
11:00 A.M.–12:00 P.M.		
12:00 P.M.–1:00 P.M.		
1:00 P.M.–2:00 P.M.		
2:00 P.M.–3:00 P.M.		
3:00 P.M.–4:00 P.M.		
4:00 P.M.–5:00 P.M.		
5:00 P.M.–6:00 P.M.		
6:00 P.M.–7:00 P.M.		
7:00 P.M.–8:00 P.M.		
8:00 P.M.–9:00 P.M.		
9:00 P.M.–10:00 P.M.		
10:00 P.M.–11:00 P.M.		
11:00 P.M.–12:00 A.M.		
12:00 A.M.–1:00 A.M.		
1:00 A.M.–2:00 A.M.		

Total Time Spent on Homework

DAILY TASK BREAKDOWN

TASK	PRIORITY (1–4)	TIME NEEDED

It's good to aim for that A+ on every assignment but remember that perfect can be the enemy of good. If you've been tracking your overall grade in a class (see p. TK), you should know where you need to put in that extra effort and where you might be able to ease off, if needed.

✏ DAILY PLANNER

Day _____	Classes	Homework
7:00 A.M.–8:00 A.M.		
8:00 A.M.–9:00 A.M.		
9:00 A.M.–10:00 A.M.		
10:00 A.M.–11:00 A.M.		
11:00 A.M.–12:00 P.M.		
12:00 P.M.–1:00 P.M.		
1:00 P.M.–2:00 P.M.		
2:00 P.M.–3:00 P.M.		
3:00 P.M.–4:00 P.M.		
4:00 P.M.–5:00 P.M.		
5:00 P.M.–6:00 P.M.		
6:00 P.M.–7:00 P.M.		
7:00 P.M.–8:00 P.M.		
8:00 P.M.–9:00 P.M.		
9:00 P.M.–10:00 P.M.		
10:00 P.M.–11:00 P.M.		
11:00 P.M.–12:00 A.M.		
12:00 A.M.–1:00 A.M.		
1:00 A.M.–2:00 A.M.		

**Total Time Spent
on Homework**

DAILY TASK BREAKDOWN

TASK	PRIORITY (1–4)	TIME NEEDED

Follow up on your tests and assignments. Missed questions are an opportunity for future growth, and you should make sure you understand what you got wrong so that next time you get it right.

✎ DAILY PLANNER

Day _____	Classes	Homework
7:00 A.M.–8:00 A.M.		
8:00 A.M.–9:00 A.M.		
9:00 A.M.–10:00 A.M.		
10:00 A.M.–11:00 A.M.		
11:00 A.M.–12:00 P.M.		
12:00 P.M.–1:00 P.M.		
1:00 P.M.–2:00 P.M.		
2:00 P.M.–3:00 P.M.		
3:00 P.M.–4:00 P.M.		
4:00 P.M.–5:00 P.M.		
5:00 P.M.–6:00 P.M.		
6:00 P.M.–7:00 P.M.		
7:00 P.M.–8:00 P.M.		
8:00 P.M.–9:00 P.M.		
9:00 P.M.–10:00 P.M.		
10:00 P.M.–11:00 P.M.		
11:00 P.M.–12:00 A.M.		
12:00 A.M.–1:00 A.M.		
1:00 A.M.–2:00 A.M.		

Total Time Spent on Homework

DAILY TASK BREAKDOWN

TASK	PRIORITY (1–4)	TIME NEEDED

Every student has their own strengths and weaknesses. You can improve your best areas by helping those who are struggling, and you should feel comfortable reaching out to others for help.

✎ DAILY PLANNER

Day _____		
	Classes	**Homework**
7:00 A.M.–8:00 A.M.		
8:00 A.M.–9:00 A.M.		
9:00 A.M.–10:00 A.M.		
10:00 A.M.–11:00 A.M.		
11:00 A.M.–12:00 P.M.		
12:00 P.M.–1:00 P.M.		
1:00 P.M.–2:00 P.M.		
2:00 P.M.–3:00 P.M.		
3:00 P.M.–4:00 P.M.		
4:00 P.M.–5:00 P.M.		
5:00 P.M.–6:00 P.M.		
6:00 P.M.–7:00 P.M.		
7:00 P.M.–8:00 P.M.		
8:00 P.M.–9:00 P.M.		
9:00 P.M.–10:00 P.M.		
10:00 P.M.–11:00 P.M.		
11:00 P.M.–12:00 A.M.		
12:00 A.M.–1:00 A.M.		
1:00 A.M.–2:00 A.M.		

**Total Time Spent
on Homework**

DAILY TASK BREAKDOWN

TASK	PRIORITY (1–4)	TIME NEEDED

See how other students go about solving their homework. The way they model a problem or set up their environment could be of use to you; there's always room for improvement.

✎ DAILY PLANNER

Day _____		
	Classes	**Homework**
7:00 A.M.–8:00 A.M.		
8:00 A.M.–9:00 A.M.		
9:00 A.M.–10:00 A.M.		
10:00 A.M.–11:00 A.M.		
11:00 A.M.–12:00 P.M.		
12:00 P.M.–1:00 P.M.		
1:00 P.M.–2:00 P.M.		
2:00 P.M.–3:00 P.M.		
3:00 P.M.–4:00 P.M.		
4:00 P.M.–5:00 P.M.		
5:00 P.M.–6:00 P.M.		
6:00 P.M.–7:00 P.M.		
7:00 P.M.–8:00 P.M.		
8:00 P.M.–9:00 P.M.		
9:00 P.M.–10:00 P.M.		
10:00 P.M.–11:00 P.M.		
11:00 P.M.–12:00 A.M.		
12:00 A.M.–1:00 A.M.		
1:00 A.M.–2:00 A.M.		

Total Time Spent on Homework

Chapter 5

Weekly Planner

The weekly planner is a good bridge between your day-to-day and overall monthly assignments. It's here, where deadlines are a bit further out, that you'll have more wiggle room for spreading tasks out, and your future self will thank you for not putting it all off to the weekend.

WEEKLY PROJECT BREAKDOWN

The one benefit of daily assignments is that they're, well, daily: there's no question as to when they're due. (Tomorrow!) Of course, if you only ever focus on the work that's due the next day, you'll wind up having to cram in work on projects that aren't designed to be finished in a single night. This can lead to sloppy, unfinished work and, worse, seriously stress you out.

As with the day planners from Chapter 4, the trick is to estimate how long you expect a project to take and then break it into more manageable chunks. You'll also want to adapt along the way. If you think an assignment will take six hours and you split it into three equal two-hour chunks, and then the first part takes three hours, adjust your expectations.

Use a sample table like the one below to map out each long-term project, then slot it into your weekly planner.

PROJECT	DUE	PARTS	TIME
History Paper: How Was the West "Won"?	11/17	Research: Gather Four Sources	60 minutes
		Source 1: Get Three Quotes	30 minutes
		Source 2: Get Three Quotes	30 minutes
		Source 3: Get Three Quotes	30 minutes
		Source 4: Get Three Quotes	30 minutes
		Pre-Writing: Draft Quotes into Paper	90 minutes
		Writing: Answer Every Question	90 minutes
TOTAL TIME			6 hours

After you're done, be sure to transfer each component to a specific part of your daily planner—treat it like you would any other homework assignment that's due the next day. (Unless it's *actually* due the next day, you can make these less of a priority than others, but don't get in the habit of doing so, or you'll never finish.)

If you left yourself any notes about modifications to a project, make sure you transfer those to the daily notes as well. It doesn't do you any good to know that the bridge is out ahead when driving if you keep speeding right toward it.

You may also note that Saturday and Sunday are shaded off, similarly to how evening hours were in the day planner. This isn't recommending that you don't work at all on the weekend. You should, however, aim to keep a balanced schedule that works for you. Be kind to your future self and don't schedule everything for the weekend or, worse, Sunday evening.

✏️ WEEKLY PLANNER

Week _____		
Weekday	**Project**	**Modifications**
Monday		
Tuesday		
Wednesday		
Thursday		
Friday		
Saturday		
Sunday		

WEEKLY PROJECT BREAKDOWN

Use the right-hand margin of these planners to leave notes for yourself about work that you've completed. If you're spending so much time on long-term work that you run out of time to do the material that's due tomorrow, shift future scheduling around. If you find a specific task to be a refreshing break from other work, put it between grueling tasks. Make the routine work for you!

PROJECT	DUE	PARTS	TIME
TOTAL TIME			

If you've got a lot to read, it can be very helpful to spread it out throughout the week. However, don't just constantly start and stop—that can be jarring and make it harder to retain information. Try to get through complete thoughts or sections that you can then digest between readings.

✐ WEEKLY PLANNER

Week _____		
Weekday	**Project**	**Modifications**
Monday		
Tuesday		
Wednesday		
Thursday		
Friday		
Saturday		
Sunday		

WEEKLY PROJECT BREAKDOWN

Break down any new project for the week in the table below, and then transfer those chunks to your calendar. Remember to use the modifications column to help adjust your estimates and planning for the project.

PROJECT	DUE	PARTS	TIME
TOTAL TIME			

Reading isn't just about making it from the top of the page to the end of it; it's about understanding what you've read. Especially if you're in a distracting environment, take a break every few pages—more often, if needed—and ask yourself a question about what you've read.

✏️ WEEKLY PLANNER

Week _____		
Weekday	**Project**	**Modifications**
Monday		
Tuesday		
Wednesday		
Thursday		
Friday		
Saturday		
Sunday		

WEEKLY PROJECT BREAKDOWN

PROJECT	DUE	PARTS	TIME
TOTAL TIME			

If you're having trouble focusing on the reading (and you can't remove the distraction), try being more active by taking meaningful notes. That doesn't mean just highlight every other word—instead, engage with the underlying ideas. When you're done with a section, gather up the most critical notes so that it's easier to pick up where you left off.

✏️ WEEKLY PLANNER

Week _____		
Weekday	**Project**	**Modifications**
Monday		
Tuesday		
Wednesday		
Thursday		
Friday		
Saturday		
Sunday		

WEEKLY PROJECT BREAKDOWN

PROJECT	DUE	PARTS	TIME
TOTAL TIME			

You might not understand everything as you read it the first time and might not be able to look things up or ask others for more details. Find a way to flag those trouble spots and make a point of coming back to them later, well before your homework is due.

✎ WEEKLY PLANNER

Week _____		
Weekday	**Project**	**Modifications**
Monday		
Tuesday		
Wednesday		
Thursday		
Friday		
Saturday		
Sunday		

WEEKLY PROJECT BREAKDOWN

PROJECT	DUE	PARTS	TIME
TOTAL TIME			

Don't act aimlessly. Whether you're reading or writing, know exactly what you're hoping to achieve in that session. For your own sake, choose achievable goals—don't add unnecessary pressure by trying to write an entire paper in one sitting (unless you've done so before, and the timing works out for you).

✏️ WEEKLY PLANNER

Week _____		
Weekday	**Project**	**Modifications**
Monday		
Tuesday		
Wednesday		
Thursday		
Friday		
Saturday		
Sunday		

WEEKLY PROJECT BREAKDOWN

PROJECT	DUE	PARTS	TIME
TOTAL TIME			

Unless your assignment is due tomorrow and there are no extensions, it's okay to not finish your work in the time you've allotted. Just make sure you leave yourself a brief note of where to pick things up so you don't miss a beat.

✐ WEEKLY PLANNER

Week _____		
Weekday	**Project**	**Modifications**
Monday		
Tuesday		
Wednesday		
Thursday		
Friday		
Saturday		
Sunday		

WEEKLY PROJECT BREAKDOWN

PROJECT	DUE	PARTS	TIME
TOTAL TIME			

Before you start working and set a timer for when to stop and start the <u>next</u> assignment, note when that upcoming project is due. If it's not due tomorrow and you get into a groove with your current work, you may find it more efficient to stick with your current task. Just make sure you reallocate that time the next day.

✏️ WEEKLY PLANNER

Week _____		
Weekday	**Project**	**Modifications**
Monday		
Tuesday		
Wednesday		
Thursday		
Friday		
Saturday		
Sunday		

WEEKLY PROJECT BREAKDOWN

PROJECT	DUE	PARTS	TIME
TOTAL TIME			

If you have a habit of running over, or you're getting stressed by moving directly from one subject to the next, consider putting in buffer time for yourself. Just as you're supposed to give your eyes a rest after every hour of television you watch, so too might you want to give your brain a brief break between assignments.

✐ WEEKLY PLANNER

Week _____		
Weekday	**Project**	**Modifications**
Monday		
Tuesday		
Wednesday		
Thursday		
Friday		
Saturday		
Sunday		

WEEKLY PROJECT BREAKDOWN

PROJECT	DUE	PARTS	TIME
TOTAL TIME			

Stay positive about the work you're accomplishing instead of dwelling on everything you may still need to do. Instead of focusing on what you <u>could</u> have done, make sure you take active steps to <u>actually</u> do those things when you next resume this project.

✎ WEEKLY PLANNER

Week _____		
Weekday	**Project**	**Modifications**
Monday		
Tuesday		
Wednesday		
Thursday		
Friday		
Saturday		
Sunday		

Chapter 6

Monthly Planner

Now that you've planned things on a daily and weekly basis, take things to the next level with a monthly planner that gives you the big picture on what's coming down the road. Some teachers are better than others about overall expectations, especially at the college level, so if you have a syllabus, begin by transcribing all the known deadlines for your work into this portion of your planner. Identify the critical points where multiple long-term assignments (or exams) may be piling up and look to distribute that work as early as possible.

MONTHLY PLANNER

Whereas daily projects can simply be scheduled for that night and completed in one go, and weekly projects can usually be chunked by the total number of hours across a few of your lighter days, long-term projects require a different approach. You still want to break things down, but it may be hard to do so as granularly, at least not until you've actively started working on the project. What you can do, however, is set a series of milestones—the big moments by which you *roughly* want to have work completed. And instead of doing this by hour or day, you'll likely be doing this by week if not month (you can always break down the milestone goals into smaller pieces, as you did in the previous chapter). The following table may be helpful:

Class	Topic	Due Date
English	Book Report	11/15
Milestone 1: Read the entire book		10/15
Objective 1: Decide on the main theme		10/17
Objective 2: Note the main characters		10/19
Milestone 2: Write the outline		10/23
Objective 1: Notes on the introduction and conclusion		10/27
Objective 2: Gather evidence to support theme		10/30

Start every assignment with a positive attitude. This can affect your focus and ability to comprehend the material. Remember this as you plan out and look ahead at a month's work of content, and stay calm.

✎ MONTHLY PLANNER

Month _____						
S	**M**	**T**	**W**	**T**	**F**	**S**
☐	☐	☐	☐	☐	☐	☐
☐	☐	☐	☐	☐	☐	☐
☐	☐	☐	☐	☐	☐	☐
☐	☐	☐	☐	☐	☐	☐
☐	☐	☐	☐	☐	☐	☐
☐	☐	☐	☐	☐	☐	☐

MONTHLY PLANNER

Don't forget to give yourself some free time on your calendar as well. If you see that your days, especially your weekends, are filling up with back-to-back assignments and nonstop milestones, you may need to actually assign yourself a period of time to decompress and *not* do any work. Putting it on the schedule may seem silly, but this will allow you to ensure that everything's still getting taken care of and, if you worry that there *aren't* enough hours, consider speaking with your guidance counselor to be sure that you haven't taken on *too* much.

Class	Topic	Due Date
Milestone 1:		
Objective 1:		
Objective 2:		
Milestone 2:		
Objective 1:		
Objective 2:		

The more you do a certain type of assignment, the more familiar you will be with how long it <u>should</u> take you. Use these to set benchmarks for yourself, much like a runner. See if you can beat your own best times (without compromising the quality of your work); this will help you focus on being more efficient.

✎ MONTHLY PLANNER

Month _____						
S	**M**	**T**	**W**	**T**	**F**	**S**
☐	☐	☐	☐	☐	☐	☐
☐	☐	☐	☐	☐	☐	☐
☐	☐	☐	☐	☐	☐	☐
☐	☐	☐	☐	☐	☐	☐
☐	☐	☐	☐	☐	☐	☐
☐	☐	☐	☐	☐	☐	☐

MONTHLY PLANNER

Put any new milestone projects in the table below and transfer them accordingly to the calendar. Remember that you can break down each objective in your weekly planner, and, if needed, take *those* steps all the way back to the day planner: whatever's most efficient for you so that nothing is overlooked!

Class	Topic	Due Date
Milestone 1:		
Objective 1:		
Objective 2:		
Milestone 2:		
Objective 1:		
Objective 2:		

Even if you don't have much space at home to get your work done, you can still find ways to make that space clearer and more calming over time. Take things a step at a time and see what works.

✎ MONTHLY PLANNER

Month _____						
S	**M**	**T**	**W**	**T**	**F**	**S**
☐	☐	☐	☐	☐	☐	☐
☐	☐	☐	☐	☐	☐	☐
☐	☐	☐	☐	☐	☐	☐
☐	☐	☐	☐	☐	☐	☐
☐	☐	☐	☐	☐	☐	☐
☐	☐	☐	☐	☐	☐	☐

MONTHLY PLANNER

Class	Topic	Due Date
Milestone 1:		
Objective 1:		
Objective 2:		
Milestone 2:		
Objective 1:		
Objective 2:		

Have you ever thought about why bridges are as narrow as they are? That's because the wider they get, the harder they are to support and the less efficient they become at their main purpose—going from point A to B. Your homework should be like a bridge and you should make sure you're actually getting your point across <u>before</u> you start adding on anything else unnecessary.

✎ MONTHLY PLANNER

Month _____						
S	**M**	**T**	**W**	**T**	**F**	**S**
☐	☐	☐	☐	☐	☐	☐
☐	☐	☐	☐	☐	☐	☐
☐	☐	☐	☐	☐	☐	☐
☐	☐	☐	☐	☐	☐	☐
☐	☐	☐	☐	☐	☐	☐
☐	☐	☐	☐	☐	☐	☐

MONTHLY PLANNER

Class	Topic	Due Date
Milestone 1:		
Objective 1:		
Objective 2:		
Milestone 2:		
Objective 1:		
Objective 2:		

Unless you're an astronaut, you're not operating in a vacuum. Time that you thought would be available may be abruptly taken up by a rescheduled extracurricular, a job opportunity, or an urgent family obligation. Make note of how many hours were lost or displaced on a given day and add them back into your schedule for the rest of the week or month at your earliest opportunity (before you forget!).

✏ MONTHLY PLANNER

Month _____						
S	**M**	**T**	**W**	**T**	**F**	**S**
☐	☐	☐	☐	☐	☐	☐
☐	☐	☐	☐	☐	☐	☐
☐	☐	☐	☐	☐	☐	☐
☐	☐	☐	☐	☐	☐	☐
☐	☐	☐	☐	☐	☐	☐
☐	☐	☐	☐	☐	☐	☐

MONTHLY PLANNER

Class	Topic	Due Date
Milestone 1:		
Objective 1:		
Objective 2:		
Milestone 2:		
Objective 1:		
Objective 2:		

Most athletes rely on a coach and have scheduled breaks in play (or timeouts) during which they can regroup and discuss how well they've been doing. This gives them the opportunity to change a strategy that's no longer working, and you should try to take the same approach. Set a timer and, when it goes off, see what you've gotten done. If you're falling way behind, see if there's anything else you can do.

✎ MONTHLY PLANNER

Month						
S	**M**	**T**	**W**	**T**	**F**	**S**

MONTHLY PLANNER

Class	Topic	Due Date
Milestone 1:		
Objective 1:		
Objective 2:		
Milestone 2:		
Objective 1:		
Objective 2:		

If you've taken a physics class or looked at architecture—or if you've tried to carry every grocery bag at once and then had sore arms the next day—you understand a thing or two about load-bearing joints. If you put too much pressure on any one part, you risk injury, and the same goes for your homework. Distribute that work so you don't collapse!

✎ MONTHLY PLANNER

Month _____						
S	**M**	**T**	**W**	**T**	**F**	**S**
☐	☐	☐	☐	☐	☐	☐
☐	☐	☐	☐	☐	☐	☐
☐	☐	☐	☐	☐	☐	☐
☐	☐	☐	☐	☐	☐	☐
☐	☐	☐	☐	☐	☐	☐
☐	☐	☐	☐	☐	☐	☐

MONTHLY PLANNER

Class	Topic	Due Date
🚩 Milestone 1:		
⚑ Objective 1:		
⚑ Objective 2:		
🚩 Milestone 2:		
⚑ Objective 1:		
⚑ Objective 2:		

You may not know about a potential conflict when you first take on an assignment—that's why it's important to add any major time commitments to your calendar pages as soon as you know about them. Writing these down in the same place will help remind you of other dates and give you the maximum amount of time to reschedule.

✏ MONTHLY PLANNER

Month _____						
S	**M**	**T**	**W**	**T**	**F**	**S**
☐	☐	☐	☐	☐	☐	☐
☐	☐	☐	☐	☐	☐	☐
☐	☐	☐	☐	☐	☐	☐
☐	☐	☐	☐	☐	☐	☐
☐	☐	☐	☐	☐	☐	☐
☐	☐	☐	☐	☐	☐	☐

MONTHLY PLANNER

Class	Topic	Due Date
_____	_____	_____
🚩 Milestone 1:		
🚩 Objective 1:		
🚩 Objective 2:		
🚩 Milestone 2:		
🚩 Objective 1:		
🚩 Objective 2:		

It's one thing to write down that your goal is to build a model rocket and launch it into space—and quite another to actually <u>do</u> so. Unless you're talking about a creative writing assignment, understand that once you write down a goal, you still have to put in the work to accomplish it, so make sure you're setting clear and realistic goals.

✏ MONTHLY PLANNER

Month _____						
S	**M**	**T**	**W**	**T**	**F**	**S**
☐	☐	☐	☐	☐	☐	☐
☐	☐	☐	☐	☐	☐	☐
☐	☐	☐	☐	☐	☐	☐
☐	☐	☐	☐	☐	☐	☐
☐	☐	☐	☐	☐	☐	☐
☐	☐	☐	☐	☐	☐	☐

MONTHLY PLANNER

Class	Topic	Due Date
⚑ Milestone 1:		
⚐ Objective 1:		
⚐ Objective 2:		
⚑ Milestone 2:		
⚐ Objective 1:		
⚐ Objective 2:		

The more packed your schedule, the better it feels to finish projects. But don't be too quick to just set something aside. Whenever possible, give yourself time to review your work so that all your hard work doesn't end up losing points for easy errors.

✎ MONTHLY PLANNER

Month _____						
S	**M**	**T**	**W**	**T**	**F**	**S**
☐	☐	☐	☐	☐	☐	☐
☐	☐	☐	☐	☐	☐	☐
☐	☐	☐	☐	☐	☐	☐
☐	☐	☐	☐	☐	☐	☐
☐	☐	☐	☐	☐	☐	☐
☐	☐	☐	☐	☐	☐	☐

MONTHLY PLANNER

Class	Topic	Due Date
🚩 Milestone 1:		
🏳 Objective 1:		
🏳 Objective 2:		
🚩 Milestone 2:		
🏳 Objective 1:		
🏳 Objective 2:		

This cannot be stressed enough: it could be the tip on every page. Did you answer all of the parts of your assignment?

✎ MONTHLY PLANNER

Month _____						
S	**M**	**T**	**W**	**T**	**F**	**S**
☐	☐	☐	☐	☐	☐	☐
☐	☐	☐	☐	☐	☐	☐
☐	☐	☐	☐	☐	☐	☐
☐	☐	☐	☐	☐	☐	☐
☐	☐	☐	☐	☐	☐	☐
☐	☐	☐	☐	☐	☐	☐

MONTHLY PLANNER

Class	Topic	Due Date
Milestone 1:		
Objective 1:		
Objective 2:		
Milestone 2:		
Objective 1:		
Objective 2:		

Have you heard the ancient question about whether a tree that falls in the forest when nobody is around makes any sound? Or about whether a paper that ignores the main idea gets a good grade? In both cases, there's an impact whether you're listening or not.

✎ MONTHLY PLANNER

Month _____						
S	**M**	**T**	**W**	**T**	**F**	**S**
☐	☐	☐	☐	☐	☐	☐
☐	☐	☐	☐	☐	☐	☐
☐	☐	☐	☐	☐	☐	☐
☐	☐	☐	☐	☐	☐	☐
☐	☐	☐	☐	☐	☐	☐
☐	☐	☐	☐	☐	☐	☐

MONTHLY PLANNER

Class	Topic	Due Date
Milestone 1:		
Objective 1:		
Objective 2:		
Milestone 2:		
Objective 1:		
Objective 2:		

Don't put all your eggs in one digital basket. If you're relying on looking something up online but have technical difficulties with the computer or modem, make sure you still have a method for getting answers, whether that's phoning a friend or going to an alternative location (like a library). If you really get stuck, try to fill that time with upcoming work from the next few days so that if the teacher lets you make up the assignment, you have the bandwidth for it.

✎ MONTHLY PLANNER

Month _____						
S	**M**	**T**	**W**	**T**	**F**	**S**
☐	☐	☐	☐	☐	☐	☐
☐	☐	☐	☐	☐	☐	☐
☐	☐	☐	☐	☐	☐	☐
☐	☐	☐	☐	☐	☐	☐
☐	☐	☐	☐	☐	☐	☐
☐	☐	☐	☐	☐	☐	☐

Chapter 7

Subject Planner

So far, you've been putting together plans for getting your homework done on the daily, weekly, and monthly level. This chapter will focus on helping you plan for and tackle specific types of assignments more efficiently, so that you can decrease the amount of time they'll take.

PERSONALIZING YOUR PROJECTS

Homework comes in various shapes and sizes, so there's no one-size-fits-all approach on an assignment-by-assignment basis. There are, however, certain things that can be very useful to track for specific types of classes. These first two pages highlight some general elements you may want to use, while the following pages give more specific ones. Your goal is to mix and match these elements, so reproduce them at whatever size is helpful to you and sketch them as roughly as needed so that you fill your perfect planner page with the things most helpful for *you* to track.

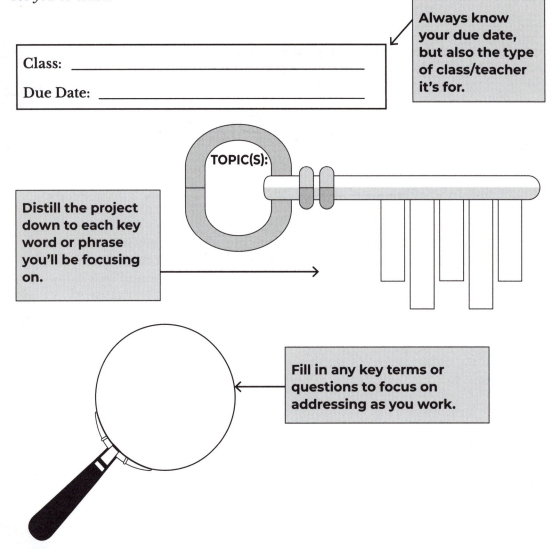

Always know your due date, but also the type of class/teacher it's for.

Class: _____

Due Date: _____

TOPIC(S):

Distill the project down to each key word or phrase you'll be focusing on.

Fill in any key terms or questions to focus on addressing as you work.

Jot down any issues you've previously had with this type of assignment so that you can avoid them.

Make sure you're doing exactly what the teacher has asked for and that you have the right resources on hand for it.

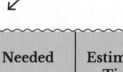

Assignment	Location	Materials Needed	Estimated Time

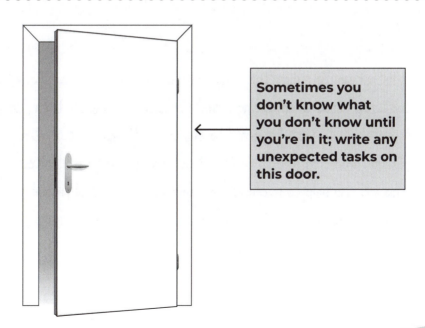

Sometimes you don't know what you don't know until you're in it; write any unexpected tasks on this door.

PREPARATION AND ORGANIZATION

Math classes are likely to give you problem sets to solve. Pay attention to any specific instructions about how teachers want you to show work, especially if they want you to solve a problem using a particular formula or method. If a tool like a protractor or graphing calculator is required, make sure you know how to use it.

 Fill in any rules, formulas, or calculator inputs that are relevant to this assignment as a quick reference guide. If, as you solve, you come up with any new techniques or are reminded of any older ones that you need, write them down as well. You can save these assignment sheets by topic and use them to build out flashcards before a test.

 On each empty line, write down the number of a question you've been assigned. If there isn't enough room to list all of the problems, add more checkboxes or get a separate sheet of paper. Check off each one as you solve it, and then check the second box once you've *reviewed* it. This will make sure you don't accidentally skip a problem or lose points by submitting a wrong answer.

Whether you're submitting your work or not, for your <u>own</u> benefit, don't skip steps when solving a math problem. The easiest way to fix a mistake is to work backward to see where things went off track, but you won't be able to do this if you haven't written it all out. This will also help to reinforce each given mathematical procedure in your mind so that you become more efficient at recalling and performing it in the future, especially on timed tests.

✏ MATH WORKSHEET

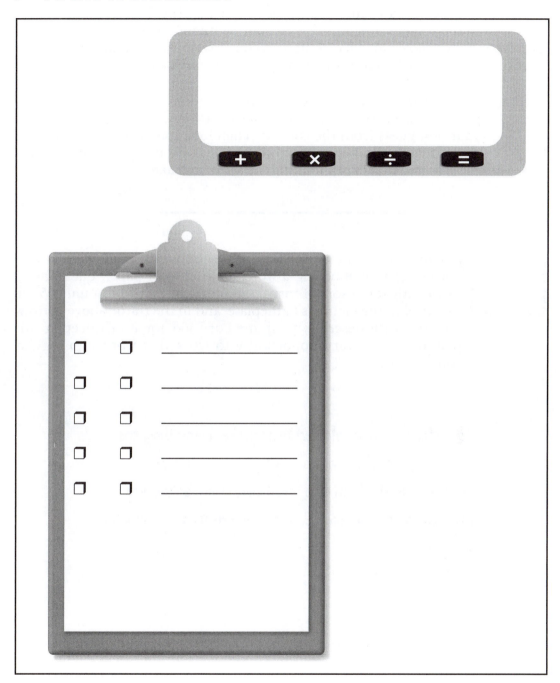

TIMELESS TOOLS

Language homework can come in a variety of forms, especially as you get more advanced in the subject. You'll likely start out by memorizing words and conjugations, and then move on to using them in conversation and, finally, translating. Here are some timeless tools for helping you get through a difficult assignment.

 If you're reading and hit a word that you don't know the meaning or pronunciation for, write down that word on a line here, along with your best guess from the context. Then look it up and see if you were right. If you're drawing the wrong conclusions, make sure you correct them so you don't keep making the same mistake.

 Try to forge a unique sensory connection with each word so that you're not remembering a word on a piece of paper, but rather a word with some sort of visual, auditory, or tactile stimulus. Write the word in the picture's nameplate, and in the frame above it, draw (or otherwise describe) your memory aid for it. To deepen this pathway, take every opportunity to work that word into regular conversation.

To better keep track of everything you're memorizing, try connecting each item with a specific image or place. This can also take the form of a mnemonic, where an easy-to-recall acronym, song, phrase, or rhyme can trigger associated memories.

✎ LANGUAGE/VOCAB WORKSHEET

KNOW YOUR STEPS

Science labs can be tricky because you might begin them in your class and then write up conclusions for homework. It is critical, whether you are working at school or at home, that you follow the directions of the experiment and record results as exactly as possible. Creating a checklist of each step, especially if they need to be performed on a timer, can help, much like putting a recipe into your own words so you know what you're doing before you start cooking. Organizing your findings, much like establishing a list of ingredients, will help you start compiling the final product. If you've been asked to use a specific type of graph, make sure you know how to draw and label it.

 Use this space to fill in the items (and quantities) you'll need, in the order in which you'll need them. Like a surgeon in the operating room, you don't want to have to step away from your work to find a missing tool.

 Look at your notes from the experiment, then take the essence of your key observations and put them here. Learning what's important will help you improve your focus on future assignments and should help pinpoint the elements worth discussing in your paper.

Preparation goes a long way for lab work. You don't just show up and play an instrument: you learn the music first and practice the technique. If you have time to review the assignment before it begins, do so, and ask questions then. Make sure you are comfortable with what you need to do, and rewrite instructions in your own words to be sure you know what you're doing. If you don't, and you have to make a guess mid-step, you might end up having to redo <u>everything</u> up to that point.

✏️ SCIENCE LAB WORKSHEET

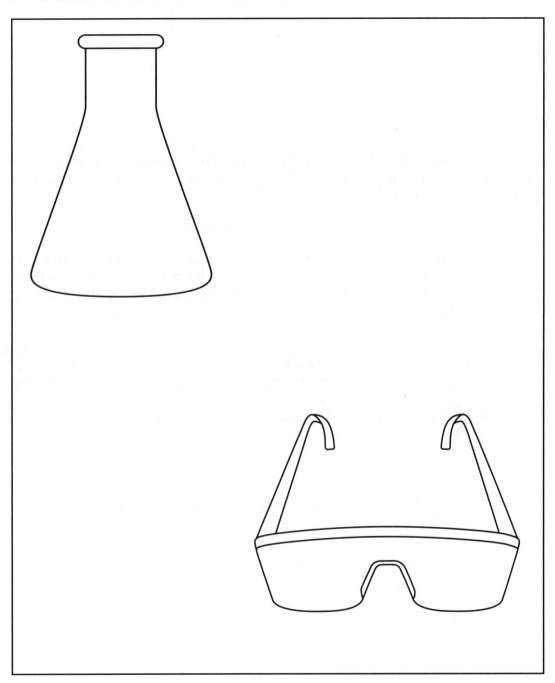

FIND YOUR SOURCES

A research paper tends to be a longer-term project, and an outline of the steps can help. If you don't have a specific topic to research, start by skimming existing material on the subject and identifying books that sound interesting to you. If you just waltz into the library, you may not gather enough information and a second trip will take way more time than a little prework.

 Before you get started, find out how the teacher wants you to cite your sources. Then, as you find material, label each book in the correct format. In the space for the pages of each book, write PRIMARY or SECONDARY depending on the type of source. Try not to have too many SECONDARY sources, and unless instructed otherwise, avoid anything that is TERTIARY.

 For each book in your stack, draw a bookmark icon and an arrow that connects it to the book. On this image, write out all the pages that you referenced: this will easily show you if you're pulling too much from a single source, especially a secondary one.

 Write your required page count (or word count) in the top of the hourglass. As you start working on drafts, update the *bottom* of the hourglass with whatever your current total is. If you're finding it difficult to get a lot done, try to split your work equally across however many days you have. If you're over, make sure you're answering the given question, and unless extra credit is up for grabs, start paring back.

Don't just leave your notes on index cards until the last minute. Putting your findings onto the page will encourage you to address their structure and cohesion and tell you if they're coming together. This first draft doesn't have to be perfect—think of it as a jigsaw puzzle, where you just want to make sure you've got the edges down so that you can connect the rest more easily.

✎ RESEARCH PAPER WORKSHEET

TIMELINES AND LANDMARKS

Many social studies assignments have to do with memorizing key facts like geographical locations, dates of battles, and historical figures. Instead of keeping this information as a bunch of flat text, try to put it in context. Organizing a timeline of events will help you better recall individual elements as well as see the bigger picture. Finding memorable details may help you better connect to and visualize terms so that they're more than words on the page.

The key structure of a timeline isn't the dates (though be sure to write those above the arrows if you're going to need them). Instead, it is in the sequence of events: what led to what. Start by filling in the most critical events closest to the timeline and if there are other pieces you need to recall or which help strengthen connections, you can draw additional branches to the left and right or even between boxes.

When time isn't as important as place, or if you're more of a visual learner, it may help you to represent what you're trying to remember on a map. Think of iconic or recognizable features of each subject and draw them as if you were filling out the map at a theme park. Draw paths between connected "landmark" moments. Fun fact: master memorizers, including the fictional Sherlock Holmes, use a similar, larger-scale method to organize their thoughts, constructing elaborate "memory palaces" that help them retrace their steps to where they "placed" each concept.

The more you write, the harder it is to memorize. Be direct and vivid: in short, be memorable. Keep it simple and uncluttered beyond what you're trying to learn, and if a small detail, like a humorously named horse, helps, use it.

✏️ HISTORY/SOCIAL STUDIES WORKSHEET

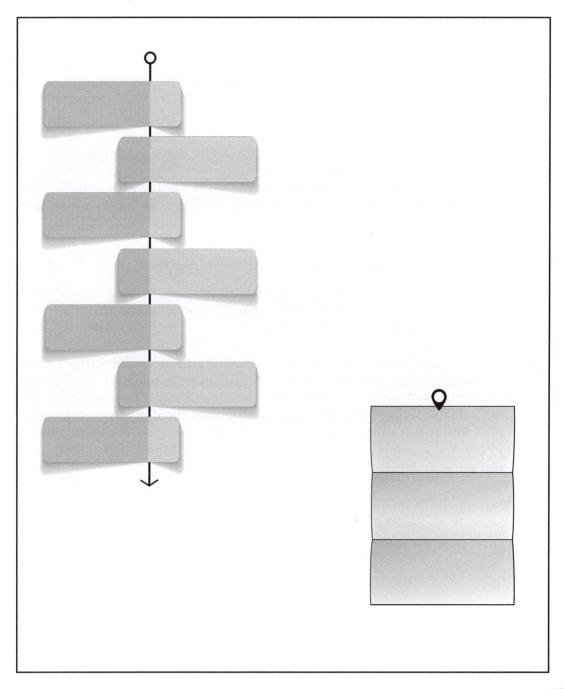

GROUP PROJECT SUCCESS

Group projects can be challenging because you are working with other people who will likely have different personalities, goals, and work habits than yours. To make sure that everyone in your group is on the same page and to pre-empt potential problems, come up with clear assignments and deadlines as a group and have each member sign off on what they're doing. Set earlier deadlines than you normally would so that if there are any problems, there's still time to course correct.

 In the left-most lobe of the brain, write down your initial "brainstorming" ideas. After talking them over with other members of your group, write their additional suggestions in the middle lobe. Finally, in the right-most lobe, refine all the ideas into a final plan that everyone can agree on.

 Use the table to break out each task. If two parts are connected, make a note of that. For each piece, write in how long you think it'll take you, and how interested you are.

Try to give everybody their first choices—if there's a tie, give the assignment to the person who thinks they can do it in less time (more efficiently). Once you've assigned everything, add up the total number of estimated hours and then plot each task on the pie chart as a percentage of that total. (So if you had 50 hours of work and a task that took 4 hours, that would be 8% of the chart.) Use this visualization to tell if any one person is taking on way more than their fair share of work.

As a final step, have each team member initial their portion and confirm when they're aiming to deliver each part.

✏️ GROUP PROJECT WORKSHEET

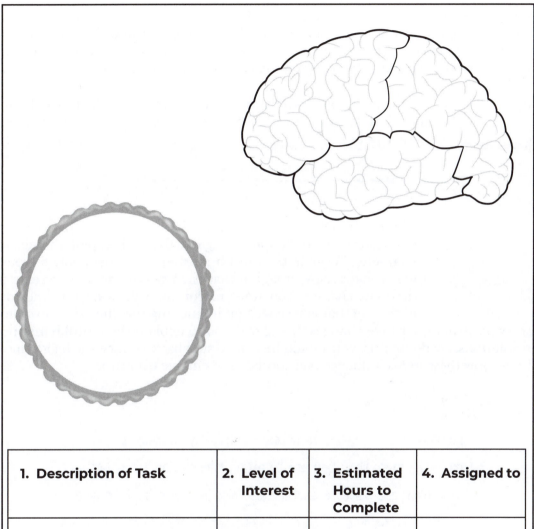

1. Description of Task	2. Level of Interest	3. Estimated Hours to Complete	4. Assigned to

FIND THE DEEPER MEANING

A book report is rarely just a plot summary. Make sure you are prepared to delve into the deeper meaning or significance of the story by actively reading. Think about the main idea, and if your teacher has provided a question or topic in advance, keep asking yourself about it at the end of each chapter. Use this worksheet to make sure you're focusing on the right supporting details.

 Write down, in your own words, what you've been asked to look for. (Putting it in your own words helps to ensure that you understand the assignment.)

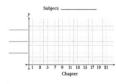 Choose the subject that you feel will best help you answer your question. This can be something like the **setting**, **plot**, **theme**, or **character**. Write in the most important ones that apply to your given focus. Now imagine that each x-axis mark represents a different chapter. You want to continue drawing the line for each item that you've written in, moving the line up or down to show positive or negative changes. Use shorthand to explain these **problems** and **resolutions**. By doing this, you should be able to step back and see the bigger picture—how these items influence one another and change over time.

The more actively you take notes—physically marking up your text—the more likely you are to retain information. Transferring it from one place to another also aids in imprinting it in your memory. Try using a pencil, pen, highlighter, or sticky notes to mark a chapter as you go, without breaking the flow of your reading. When you're done reading for the day, review what you wrote and record it in a separate place, such as in the graph on the worksheet to the right.

✎ READING WORKSHEET (BOOK REPORT)

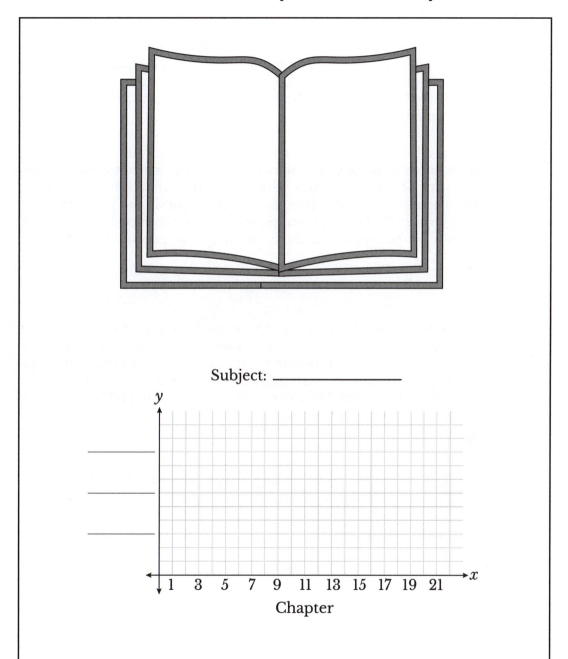

Subject: _____

SUPPORT YOUR THESIS

When writing an essay, you need to have an **introduction, body**, and **conclusion**, but you also need to make sure that they work together. If you have ever baked or eaten a layer cake, you know that each tier balances on the one beneath it, and if the cake doesn't have a sturdy base it will collapse. There are likely pieces that you can move around while still keeping a cohesive whole, but you've got to remain mindful of how it all fits together, and unlike Jenga, you don't win by writing the longest essay.

 Because a thesis statement is the basis for your essay, it can seem overwhelming to write one. Just remember that the goal of a thesis statement is to declare what your paper or essay is about, or what readers should expect. Generate some ideas for your thesis and jot them down in the light bulb. Don't choose topics that are too broad or narrow or you may not be able to find the supporting evidence that you will need.

 Now you are going to formulate your **body paragraphs**. On the top of the table, state the main idea for your essay. Then by each table leg, write the theme for that paragraph and note the supporting evidence. Generally, essays have a minimum of three body paragraphs, but you can include more (and add extra legs) if needed and if the assignment allows.

Starting is the hardest part of writing a paper. Give yourself permission to write a (mediocre / less-than-stellar / just okay) paper. Just get something down; you can edit it and make it great later.

✎ WRITING WORKSHEET (ESSAY)

MAP OUT VISUAL PRESENTATION

Physical presentations can be many things, but the most common are **dioramas** and **poster** or **foam board presentations**. However you design your presentation, make sure that the assignment question or objective has been met.

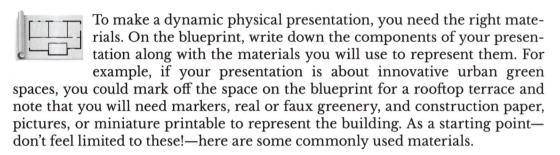 To make a dynamic physical presentation, you need the right materials. On the blueprint, write down the components of your presentation along with the materials you will use to represent them. For example, if your presentation is about innovative urban green spaces, you could mark off the space on the blueprint for a rooftop terrace and note that you will need markers, real or faux greenery, and construction paper, pictures, or miniature printable to represent the building. As a starting point—don't feel limited to these!—here are some commonly used materials.

- Found objects (rocks, twigs, leaves)
- Colored pencils, markers
- Paint
- Modeling clay
- Construction paper
- Magazines or pictures

- Fabric
- Adhesive (glue, hot glue gun, tape)
- Scissors
- Miniature printables (lots of free sites, but you will need to have access to a color printer)

Bring together all of the tools needed for the assignment. An organized workspace will make you more efficient at completing your task.

✎ PHYSICAL PRESENTATION WORKSHEET

MATERIALS

_____
_____
_____
_____
_____
_____
_____
_____
_____
_____

INCORPORATE TECHNOLOGY

The key difference between making a presentation with the assistance of technology and doing something physical is that you're not limited to a single, fixed object. As with any presentation, make the most of what's available to you, and look for ways to complement the information you're trying to share. Start by making sure you are including enough of what the teacher is asking for, whether those are audio, video, or interactive components. Once you understand *what* you need to showcase, look at the tools available to you and pick the best methods for presenting each one.

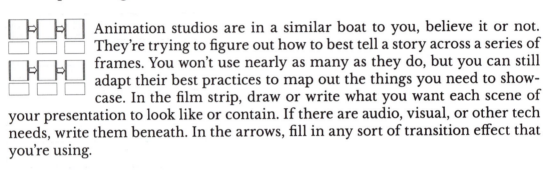 Animation studios are in a similar boat to you, believe it or not. They're trying to figure out how to best tell a story across a series of frames. You won't use nearly as many as they do, but you can still adapt their best practices to map out the things you need to showcase. In the film strip, draw or write what you want each scene of your presentation to look like or contain. If there are audio, visual, or other tech needs, write them beneath. In the arrows, fill in any sort of transition effect that you're using.

Stay within the scope of the assignment. There's no reason to create extra work when it's not part of the task. Believe it or not, the more you throw into this assignment, the more cluttered it'll get, so you might actually cost yourself points by being overzealous.

✏️ TECHNOLOGY WORKSHEET

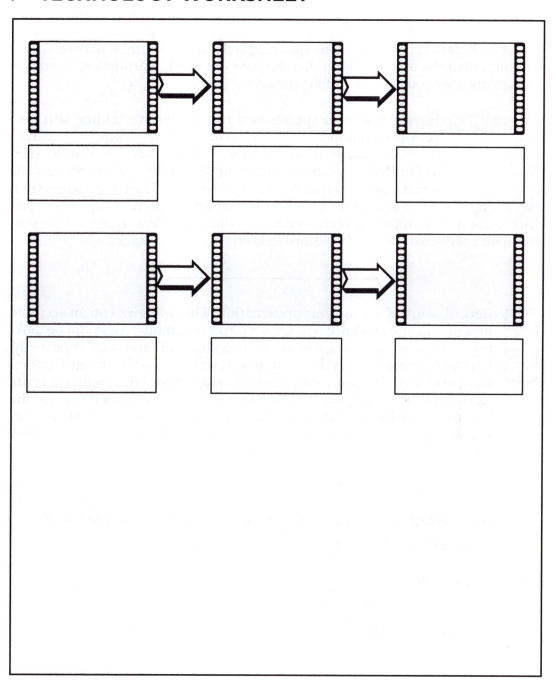

OVERCOME FEAR OF PUBLIC SPEAKING

While you need to factor in the time for researching, outlining, and writing your presentation, the stumbling block for most people is speaking in front of an audience. In fact, the fear of public speaking is the most common phobia—more common than the fear of spiders, heights, or even death. Fortunately, there are ways to mitigate your fears of public speaking.

Having a written speech or a comprehensive outline will give your presentation flow and structure, but you ultimately need to be able to give your presentation without reading it. You can start to familiarize yourself with your speech by reading aloud your written presentation, but *don't memorize* it. Trying to memorize it can be detrimental if you forget a word or phrase and then freeze up. When you are comfortable with your speech, write down the main ideas from your presentation on a notecard (e.g., bullet points) to keep yourself on track.

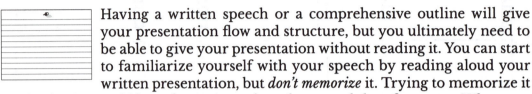

Record yourself giving your presentation. This will give you an accurate idea of how the audience will see you. You might unconsciously be looking at the floor, speaking too softly, or saying "uh" and "um" repeatedly. On the phone screen in the main boxes, write down the things that you want to change. Record your presentation again and then watch it again. In the first small box, tally the number of times that you do or say the things that are bothering you. Do this at least 2-3 more times and your performance should improve. This is a surefire strategy that athletes utilize—watching recordings of themselves to perfect their technique.

One way to combat nerves is with calming breathing techniques. A good one to try is Box Breathing, which consists of four steps. Repeat as needed.

1. Breathe in for 4 seconds
2. Hold your breath for 4 seconds
3. Breathe out for 4 seconds
4. Hold for 4 seconds

✎ ORAL PRESENTATION WORKSHEET

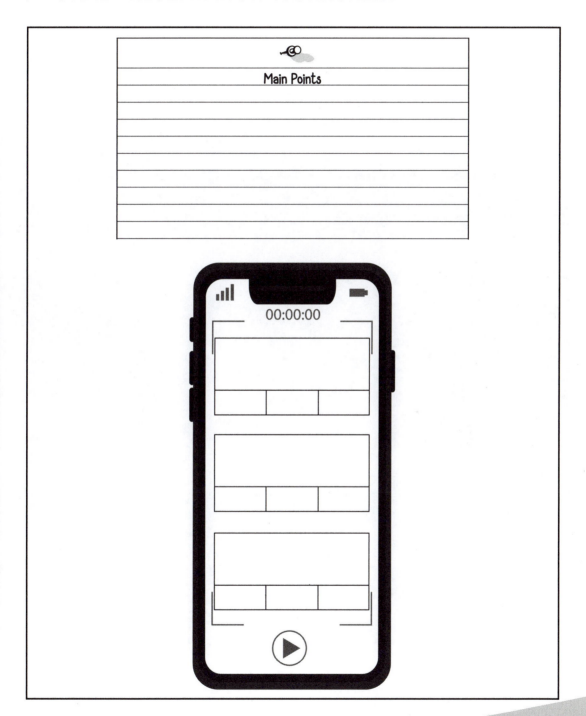

Main Points

00:00:00

Appendix
Trackers

SLEEP TRACKER

There's no one-pillow-fits-all approach to how much sleep you need. The goal of this tracker is to help you get a bigger picture of how your current sleep schedule impacts *you*, and how you might best use your time.

> If you have access to a wearable fitness app, you can try using that to log your sleep, but we recommend adding it here, too.

Begin by recording the times at which you *tried* to go to sleep and to wake up. These are the times at which you put away your book-like or phone-shaped distractions and shut off the light, and when you first opened your eyes in the morning. (Unless you woke up many times in the middle of the night or woke up for more than ten minutes, you don't need to log that.) Do the math—sorry!—and figure out how many hours that was. Write that in the middle box. To the left, put down how many minutes you lay awake, and to the right, how long you stayed in bed. These two numbers indicate where you are inefficiently using your time: if you're not falling asleep, maybe you can get a bit more work done; if you're not waking up, maybe set the alarm a bit later.

Now at the bottom of the box, try to get a sense of how you felt that day. If you felt great, check off the smiley face. If you were in a bad mood, check off the sad face. If you were falling asleep in class, check off the snorer. Once you've filled out a page of this sleep tracker, see if you can find any patterns: for instance, are you struggling to stay awake when you've had less than a certain amount of sleep? Is there a well-rested goal to aim for?

Pay particular attention to your weekend sleeping habits: are you trying to make up for the rest of the week by sleeping through the day? This is where better organizing your homework and schedule might help.

SLEEP TRACKER

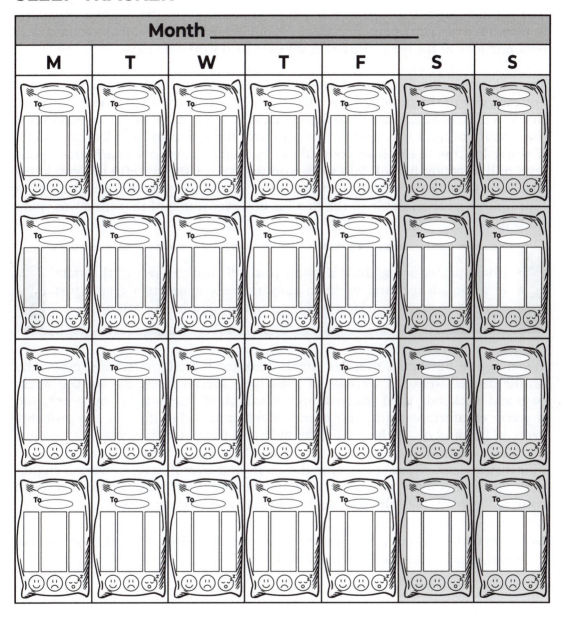

M	T	W	T	F	S	S

Month _____

WORK TRACKER

The planner pages that you've filled out elsewhere in this book are a good way to plan out what you're doing, and when, but it can also be helpful to take a step back and look at the big picture of just how much work you have.

To track your overall trends, fill out the line-and-bar graph on the next page. For each day of the month, draw a bar that represents the total amount of work that you ESTIMATED having to do on that day. Then, draw a dot that represents the amount of work you actually did. Connect these dots to complete the graph. If you're looking to improve your efficiency, you can also optionally track your level of distraction here. If you were working from 6:00 to 10:00 but you know that you were also checking texts between questions, you can put the dot at four hours and then shade in the box for however much of that time was spent off-task.

> If you prefer not to draw a graph yourself, you can record this data in a spreadsheet and use it to automatically generate a graph. Just make sure you're tracking and logging the right information.

When you've finished a month's worth, look for big picture trends, especially on the dashed weekend sections. If your lines are relatively flat for the week-days and weekends, then you're doing a great job of distributing your work, and if you're comfortable with your grades, sleep, and social life, you can probably keep on keeping on. If there's a spike here and there, identify whether you just had a lot of work (look to your estimate bars) or if something else was going on (like distractions, if you're tracking those). If your overall level of work is higher than you feel comfortable with, look at your overall class schedule: advanced courses are great, but if it's too much, you may need to step back.

Note that while this tracker is designed for your overall work trends, you can use it the same way to look at individual subjects.

WORK TRACKER

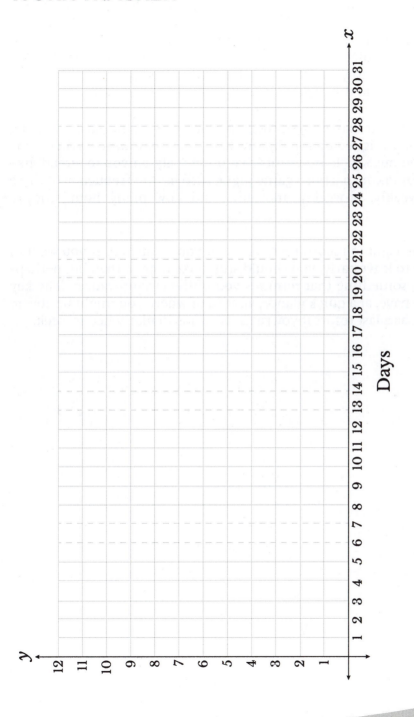

Days

COMMITMENT TRACKER

Some say that "absence makes the heart grow fonder," but when it comes to academics and extracurriculars, all it really does it hurt your reputation. That's not to say that you can't ever miss a class, but you should be aware of how often you've had to skip a club meeting. Use that information to make sure that you're participating in activities to your fullest, and to make up your mind as to when the time may have come to drop what you're no longer interested in.

In this table, list out your classes first, then any jobs you might have, then any extracurriculars you've signed up for. Finally, list other commitments that aren't officially recognized but which are events that others rely on you to attend, like watching a sibling or taking part in a game night. Also list the frequency of these activities—daily, weekly, bi-weekly, monthly—and how many hours they're scheduled for.

Use the space to the right to record each date that you've missed. If you went to an activity but had to leave early, you should still make note of that, but perhaps with an asterisk or something that reminds you of the circumstances. The key of this tracker is to have, at a quick glance, an idea of where you might be able to free up some space as a last resort if you're having a particularly hectic week.

COMMITMENT TRACKER

ACTIVITY	FREQUENCY	HOURS	DATES MISSED

GRADE TRACKER

Have you heard the expression "perfect is the enemy of good" or the concept of diminishing returns? Given an infinite number of hours, of course you'd strive to get an A+ on every assignment, and you'd study to get a 100 on each test 100% of the time! But in a world without magical time-turners, you sometimes must make the difficult decision to submit work that's just good enough. That's where this tracker comes in.

> Many school systems automatically track your grades and make this information available to you. It can still be useful to do this yourself in case there's a discrepancy or the system goes down when you need it, but you should check to see what's available online.

Write out each of your classes from most important to least important. If you're majoring in something (or planning to apply to college in a specific field), you may have a vested interest in keeping those scores as high as possible. If there's a course you want to take next year that may be impacted by a low score in a subject this year, make sure that doesn't happen. If you're uncertain, you can always speak with a faculty advisor.

In the first available box by each class, write your current score, and in the box furthest to the right, write your desired final score. Every two to three weeks, return to this tracker and update your score. Look for warning signs, like grades that are trending down for a subject. That's where you need to focus, and if you have a syllabus for that class, use it to figure out the grades you'll need to get on upcoming projects in order to raise your score enough. (If you have the time, it never hurts to ask in these situations for extra credit opportunities.)

Because the extra time that you use to get certain grades up needs to come from somewhere, you can *also* use this tracker to assess which classes you might be able to do a little less work for, so long as that doesn't negatively impact your overall GPA. These are not easy decisions to make, but they are decisions *you* should make, as opposed to just doing assignments in a random order and hoping for the best outcome.

GRADE TRACKER

CLASS	CURRENT SCORE						DESIRED SCORE

TEACHER TRACKER

The types of homework and classes aren't the only thing that changes. Who you have as a teacher matters as well, because their rules and policies can make a huge impact on your overall grade and the way in which you prioritize work.

For the star ratings, shade in anywhere from one to five pieces to demonstrate whether that value is low or high. For the YES/NO bubbles, check or shade in the one that's accurate.

Finally, in the PRO/CON habits boxes, jot down any observations about things the teacher does that are helpful (or not) for you, like how well they explain an assignment or make themselves available outside of class to answer questions.

Remember that a given teacher might not run all of their classes the same way—an honors, AP, or seminar-level course might have more stringent rules than a regular or intro-level one. Over time, you can get a sense of which teachers will be a good fit for you.

TEACHER TRACKER

Teacher:

Class: _____   **Date:** _____

Difficulty of Grading ☆

Frequency of Homework ☆

Complexity of Assignments ☆

Extra Credit Opportunities (YES) (NO)

Accepts Late Homework (YES) (NO)

HABITS	
Pro	**Con**

Sample Forms

✎ DISTRACTION BINGO

5 min.

Time to Fill Out Card

40 min.

Time to Complete Assignment

B	I	N	G	O
HUNGRY	Ate a snack	Put away (or turned off) electronics	Limited outside noise in workspace	Tidied desk
Took a relaxing stretch	Turned off social media notifications	SITTING UNCOMFORTABLY	Removed phone from my room	Closed door to my room
Organized assignments by priority	CHECKING EMAIL	★ Focus		Finished chores
	Brightened the room		Gathered all materials needed for work	WATCHING TV
	Silenced phone		SLEEPY	

NEW DISTRACTORS	HOW TO AVOID THEM
Having my cat in my room	Give her 5-10 min. of attention, then remove her from my room.

✎ READING CALCULATOR

	FICTION	TEXTBOOK	NONFICTION
	Legend	America	
	(title)	(title)	(title)
	English	U.S. History	
	(subject)	(subject)	(subject)
1. SKIMMING THE PAGE	[10] pages [4] minutes 2.5 page(s)/minute	[10] pages [8] minutes 1.25 page(s)/minute	☐ pages ☐ minutes _____ page(s)/minute
2. READING THE FULL PAGE	[10] pages [9] minutes 1.1 page(s)/minute	[10] pages [20] minutes 0.5 page(s)/minute	☐ pages ☐ minutes _____ page(s)/minute
3. ACTIVE READING	[10] pages [12] minutes 0.83 page(s)/minute	[10] pages [35] minutes 0.28 page(s)/minute	☐ pages ☐ minutes _____ page(s)/minute

Remember, to find these rates, divide the number of pages you read by the number of minutes it took.

$$\frac{\boxed{} \text{ pages}}{\boxed{} \text{ minutes}} = \underline{\quad} \text{ page(s)/minute}$$

If you've repeated this across multiple days, take the *average* of those rates by adding them together and dividing by the number of days. This will give you an increasingly accurate prediction.

✏ WRITING CALCULATOR

| Research ☰ | Pre-Writing ▦ | Writing ◩ | Editing 〰 |

Once you know how long the entire project took, shade in the percent of the whole spent on each portion; e.g., 30% + 20% + 25% + 25%.

CREATIVE WRITING   Time Spent: 1 hour

Researching: __10__ minutes   Writing: __30__ minutes

Pre-Writing: __15__ minutes   Editing: __5__ minutes

Total: __600__ words and __1.5__ pages in __60__ minutes

| 0% | 10% | 20% | 30% | 40% | 50% | 60% | 70% | 80% | 90% | 100% |

ARGUMENTATIVE WRITING   Time Spent: 5 hours

Researching: __120__ minutes   Writing: __90__ minutes

Pre-Writing: __60__ minutes   Editing: __30__ minutes

Total: __1,200__ words and __3__ pages in __300__ minutes

| 0% | 10% | 20% | 30% | 40% | 50% | 60% | 70% | 80% | 90% | 100% |

RESEARCH-BASED WRITING   Time Spent:

Researching: _____ minutes   Writing: _____ minutes

Pre-Writing: _____ minutes   Editing: _____ minutes

Total: _____ words and _____ pages in _____ minutes

| 0% | 10% | 20% | 30% | 40% | 50% | 60% | 70% | 80% | 90% | 100% |

✎ MATH CALCULATOR

TYPES OF PROBLEMS		
EASY	**MEDIUM**	**HARD**
combining integers	adding fractions	dividing fractions
order of operation	subtracting fractions	multiplying fractions
finding the area	finding the percentage	squared or cubed fractions

Calculator

					Equation Sheet
⊗	✔	1.	_3_ Minutes Taken	✗	✓
✗	✓	2.	_2_ Minutes Taken	⊗	✔
✗	✓	3.	_5_ Minutes Taken	⊗	✔
⊗	✔	4.	_5_ Minutes Taken	⊗	✔
✗	✓	5.	_2_ Minutes Taken	⊗	✔
✗	✔	6.	____ Minutes Taken	✗	✔
✗	✔	7.	____ Minutes Taken	✗	✔
✗	✔	8.	____ Minutes Taken	✗	✔
✗	✔	9.	____ Minutes Taken	✗	✔
✗	✔	10.	____ Minutes Taken	✗	✔

✎ CHECKLIST

Name of Class: English

Type of Assignment: Research paper

TASK	REQUIREMENTS	DONE
research	gather 4 sources find 7 quotes	✔
make outline	include each topic needing to be addressed	✔
write paper	1,200 words, 12pt Times New Roman font, single-spaced	
edit paper	grammar, spelling, make sure to have transition sentences	

PHYSICAL TOOLS NEEDED

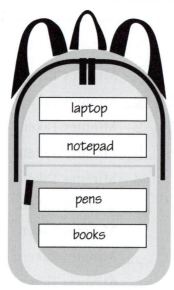

laptop

notepad

pens

books

✏️ WORKSPACE WORD SEARCH ANSWERS

R	C	C	D	I	C	T	I	O	N	A	R	Y	P
Y	E	K	T	F	A	N	R	S	N	U	D	O	M
L	T	S	K	O	O	L	A	N	N	E	T	N	R
C	E	U	E	N	K	L	E	E	S	K	P	R	C
K	T	D	R	A	H	P	D	P	S	T	O	A	R
I	A	C	C	L	R	P	N	E	U	R	L	A	E
N	C	B	O	A	P	C	D	N	R	C	S	T	N
O	C	E	O	M	C	C	H	R	U	L	T	T	E
T	M	N	E	P	O	T	E	L	I	A	P	T	P
E	R	A	S	E	R	T	A	C	L	D	O	L	R
S	K	O	O	B	N	T	N	S	N	A	T	P	A
L	E	S	O	I	O	E	E	L	R	U	P	I	H
P	N	D	R	R	P	K	K	T	O	Y	A	R	S
H	K	P	O	R	E	L	P	A	T	S	L	O	I

Provided Words	Missing Words	Images
DICTIONARY	Folder	
DESKTOP	Eraser	
NOTES	Calculator	
PENS	Stapler	
RESEARCH	Sharpener	

✎ KNOW YOUR STRENGTHS

Strengths

note-taking, reading, organizing

Interests

English, History

PRIORITY	POINTS	ASSIGNMENTS	TIME
3	7	English paper - 600 words	1 hr
2	9	Math problems 1-10	45 min
1	5	Spanish - finish class assignment	10 min

Time

1. Due soon, low impact

2. Due soon, high impact

3. Due now, low impact

4. Due now, high impact

Stress

1. Do it in my sleep

2. Need a little focus

3. Need a lot of focus

4. Struggling with subject

Organization

1. Can do at school

2. Can do on commute

3. Can do at home

4. Must do at library/ other

✏️ BALANCE YOUR WEAKNESSES

Teacher: D. Kelley   **Subject:** Algebra

Assignment Date: Nov. 10   **Score:** 81%

TYPE	ERRORS	WAYS TO IMPROVE
3	didn't simplify fractions	simplify when mult or div
3	~~incorrect denominator~~	~~find lowest common denom~~
1	calculation error	double checks calcs
3	~~incomplete answer~~	~~show all work~~
1	~~wrong measurement type~~	~~copy names correctly~~
4	~~guessed answer~~	~~memorize order of operations~~
4	~~wrong answer~~	~~study ch. 4~~

19	*Total*
2	*Class Score*

9.5   4

✏ BUILD A PROJECT WORKSHEET

Project: Research presentation with slideshow

Due Date: October 15

Team Members: Emma, James, Aaron, Kate

Outside Contributors: Professor Stevens

Reservations Needed: study room in the library, computer lab

Materials Needed: class notes, library computer or laptop, smartphone for recording

Chunk	Order	Assigned Team Member	Deadline
gather images	2	Kate	Sept. 30
research	1	James, Emma	Sept. 20
interview Dr. Stevens	3	Aaron	Sept. 30
produce slideshow	4	Aaron	Oct. 10
write introduction	5	Kate	Oct. 10

Meeting Dates	Reservation Dates	Appointments	
		Contact	Time
Sept. 10	reserve study rm in lib for all mtgs	Dr. Stevens	9/07, 9:30 am
Sept. 20	computer lab: Sept. 15		
Sept. 30			
Oct. 8			
Oct. 14			

✏ NEED TO KNOW SHEET

Name of Class _____History_____

SUBJECT OR TOPIC	NEED TO KNOW
Civil War duration	1861–1865
Civil War turning point	Battle of Gettysburg
reason for the war	slavery
start of the war	Battle of Fort Sumter
Emancipation Proclamation	Jan. 1, 1863, Lincoln's executive order to free slaves in the Confederacy
last major battle	Battle of Appomattox

✎ SAMPLE FLASHCARDS

Put a check here if you've mastered this card.

Identify one specific thing you want to remember or answer. Create additional cards for any other topics, related or not.

FRONT

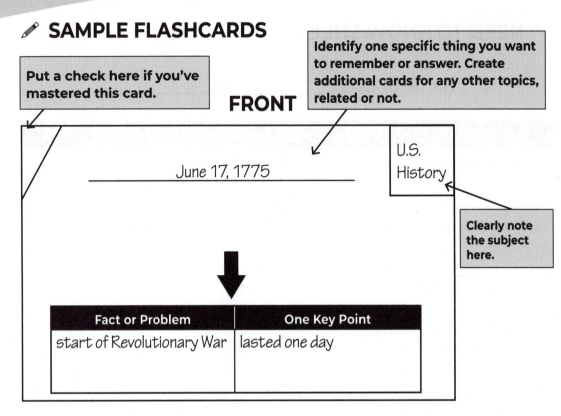

June 17, 1775

U.S. History

Clearly note the subject here.

Fact or Problem	One Key Point
start of Revolutionary War	lasted one day

BACK

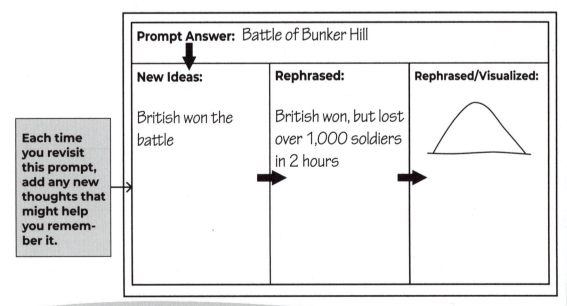

Each time you revisit this prompt, add any new thoughts that might help you remember it.

Prompt Answer: Battle of Bunker Hill

New Ideas:	Rephrased:	Rephrased/Visualized:
British won the battle	British won, but lost over 1,000 soldiers in 2 hours	

✐ POST MORTEM

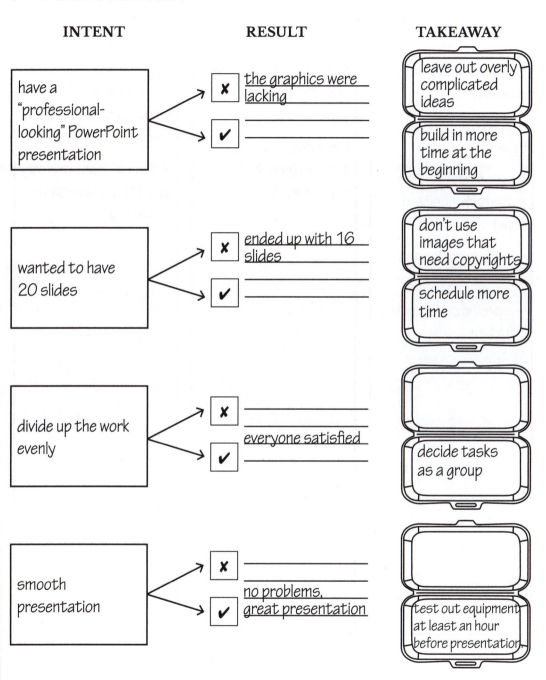

INTENT	RESULT	TAKEAWAY

INTENT: have a "professional-looking" PowerPoint presentation

RESULT: ✗ the graphics were lacking / ✔ ___

TAKEAWAY: leave out overly complicated ideas / build in more time at the beginning

INTENT: wanted to have 20 slides

RESULT: ✗ ended up with 16 slides / ✔ ___

TAKEAWAY: don't use images that need copyrights / schedule more time

INTENT: divide up the work evenly

RESULT: ✗ ___ / ✔ everyone satisfied

TAKEAWAY: decide tasks as a group

INTENT: smooth presentation

RESULT: ✗ ___ / ✔ no problems, great presentation

TAKEAWAY: test out equipment at least an hour before presentation

✎ BE THE TEACHER

Prework	Draft	Grading
Peer Review English assignment —read classmate's paper —write critique (one paragraph, positive tone) —edit grammar and spelling —specific constructive criticism	add at least two more ways to improve the paper point out what's positive (genuine compliment)	Be more specific, detailed with constructive criticisms and with compliments Include at least one way you felt a connection to the story